I0213316

THE DAREDEVIL

Maria Thompson Daviess

1st WORLD
LIBRARY
Literary Society

The Daredevil

Maria Thompson Daviess

© 1st World Library – Literary Society, 2005
PO Box 2211
Fairfield, IA 52556
www.1stworldlibrary.org
First Edition

LCCN: 2004195650

Softcover ISBN: 1-4218-0472-7
Hardcover ISBN: 1-4218-0372-0
eBook ISBN: 1-4218-0572-3

Purchase *"The Daredevil"*
as a traditional bound book at:
www.1stWorldLibrary.org/purchase.asp?ISBN=1-4218-0472-7

1st World Library Literary Society is a nonprofit
organization dedicated to promoting literacy by:

- Creating a free internet library accessible from any
  computer worldwide.
- Hosting writing competitions and offering book
  publishing scholarships.

CONTENTS

CHAPTER I

SPARKLING WAVES OVER HIGH EXPLOSIVES

Was there ever a woman who did not very greatly desire for herself, at long moments, the doublet and hose of a man, perhaps also his sword, as well as his attitude in the viewing of life? I think not. To a very small number of those ladies of great curiosity it has been granted that they climb to those ramparts of the life of a man; but it was needful that they be stout of limb and sturdy of heart to sustain themselves upon that eminence and not be dashed below upon the rocks of a strange land. I, Roberta, Marquise de Grez and Bye, have obtained glimpses into a far country and this is what I bring on returning, not as a spy, but, shall I say, laden with spices and forbidden fruit?

And for me it has been a very fine dash into the wilds of a land of strangeness, and I do not know that I have yet found myself completely returned unto my estate of a woman.

I first began to realize that I was set out upon a great journey when I stood at the rail of the very large ship and watched it plow its way through the waves which they told us with their splendor hid cruel mines. I felt the future might be like unto those great waves, and it might be that it would break in sparkling crests over high explosives. I found them!

I had seen a fear of those explosives of life come in my dying father's eyes, and here I stood at his command out on the ocean in quest of a woman's fate in a strange country.

"Get back to America, Bob, and go straight to your Uncle Robert at Hayesville in the Harpeth Valley. He cut me loose because he didn't understand, when I married your mother out of the French opera in Paris. When I named you Roberta for him he returned the letter I sent but with a notice of a thousand dollars in Monroe and Company for you. I didn't tell him when your mother died. God, I've been bitter! But these German bullets have cut the life out of me and I see more plainly. Get the money and take Nannette and the kiddie on the first boat. There's starvation and - maybe worse in Paris for you. Take - the money - and - get - to - brother Robert. God of America - take - them and - guide -"

And that was all. I held him in my arms for a long time, while old Nannette and small Pierre wept beside me, and then I laid him upon his pillow and straightened the little tricolor that the good Sister of the old gray convent in which he lay had given me to place in his hand when he had begged for it. My mother's country had meant my mother to him and he had given his life for her and France in the trenches of the Vosges. And thus at his bidding I was on the very high seas of adventure. From this thought of him I was very suddenly recalled by old Nannette who came upon the deck from below.

"*Le bon Dieu*," she sighed, as she settled herself in her

Maria Thompson Daviess

steamer chair and took out the lace knitting. "Is it not of a goodness that I have tied in my stocking the necessary francs that we may land in that America, where all is of such a good fortune? And also by my skill we have one hundred and fifty francs above that need which must be almost an hundred of their huge and wasteful dollars. All is well with us." And as she spoke she pulled up the collar of Pierre's soft blue serge blouse around his pale thin face and eased the cushion behind his crooked small back.

"Is - is that all which remains of the fifteen hundred dollars we found to be in that bank, Nannette?" I asked of her with a great uncertainty. My mother's fortune, descended from her father, the Marquis de Grez and Bye, and the income of my father from his government post, had made life easy to live in that old house by the Quay, where so many from the Faubourg St. Germaine came to hear her sing after her fortune and children took her from the Opera - and to go for the summers in the gray old Chateau de Grez - but of the investment of francs or dollars and cents I had no knowledge, in spite of my claims to be an American girl of much progress. My mother had laughed and very greatly adored my assumption of an extreme American manner, copied as nearly as possible after that of my father, and had failed to teach to me even that thrift which is a part of the dot of every French girl from the Faubourg St. Germaine to the Boulevard St. Michel. But even in my ignorance the information of Nannette as to the smallness of our fortune gave to me an alarm.

"What will you, Mademoiselle? It was necessary that I purchase the raiment needful to the young Marquis de Grez according to his state, and for the Marquise his sister also. It was not to be contemplated that we should travel except in apartments of the very best in the ship. Is not gold enough in America even for sending in great sums for relief of suffering? Have I not seen it given in the streets of Paris? Is it not there for us? Do you make me reproaches?" And Nannette began to weep into the fine lawn of her nurse's handkerchief.

"No, no, Nannette; I know it was of a necessity to us to have the clothes, and of course we had to travel in the first class. Do not have distress. If we need more money in America I will obtain it." I made that answer with a gesture of soothing upon her old shoulders which I could never remember as not bent in an attitude of hovering over Pierre or me.

"*Eh bien!*" she answered with a perfect satisfaction at my assumption of all the responsibilities of our three existences.

And as I leaned against the deck rail and looked out into a future as limitless as that water ahead of us into which the great ship was plowing, I made a remark to myself that had in it all the wisdom of those who are ignorant.

"The best of life is not to know what will happen next."

"Ah, that was so extraordinary coming from a woman that you must pardon me for listening and making exclamation," came an answer in a nice voice near at my elbow. The words were spoken in as perfect English as I had learned from my father, but in them I observed to be an intonation that my French ear detected as Parisian. "Also, Mademoiselle, are you young women of the new era to be without that very delightful but often danger-creating quality of curiosity?" As I turned I looked with startled eyes into the grave face of a man less than forty years, whose sad eyes were for the moment lighting with a great tenderness which I did not understand.

"I believe the quality which will be most required of the women of the era which is mine, is - is courage and then more courage, Monsieur," I made answer to him as if I had been discussing some question with him in my father's smoking room at the Chateau de Grez, as I often came in to do with my father and his friends after the death of my mother when the evenings seemed too long alone. They had liked that I so came at times, and the old Count de Breaux once had remarked that feminine sympathy was the flux with which men made solid their minds into a unanimous purpose. He had been speaking of that war a few weeks after Louvaine and I had risen and had stood very tall and very haughty before him and my father.

"The women of France are to come after this carnage to mold a nation from what remains to them, Monsieur," I had said to him as I looked straight into his face. "Is not the courage of women a war supply upon which to rely?"

"God! what are the young women - such women as she - going to do in the years that come after the deluge, Henri of America?" he had made a muttering question to my father as his old eyes smouldered over me in the fire-light.

From the memory of the smoking room at the Chateau de Grez my mind suddenly returned to the rail of the ship and the Frenchman beside me, who was looking into my face with the same kindly question as to my future that had been in the eyes of my old godfather and which had stirred my father's heart to its American depths and made him send me back to his own country.

"Ah, yes, that courage is a good weapon with which to adventure in this America of the Grizzled Bear, Mademoiselle," I found the strange man saying to me with a nice amusement as well as interest.

"My father had shot seven grizzlies before his twenty-first birthday. We have the skins, four of them, in the great hall of the Chateau de Grez - or - or we did have them before - before -" My voice faltered and I could not continue speaking for the tears that rose in my throat and eyes.

Quickly the man at my side turned his broad shoulders so that he should shield me from the laughing and exclaiming groups of people upon the deck near us.

"Before Ypres, Mademoiselle?" he asked with tears also in the depths of his voice.

"Yes," I answered. "And I am now going into the great America with my crippled brother and his nurse - alone. It is the land of my father and I have his courage - I *must* have also that of a French woman. I have it, Monsieur," and as I spoke I drew myself to my full, broad-shouldered height, which was almost equal to that of the man beside me.

"Mademoiselle, I salute the courage born of an American who fought before the guns of the Marne and of a French woman who sent him there!" And as he spoke thus he removed from his head his silk deck cap and held it at his shoulder in a way that I knew was a salute from a French officer to the memory of a brother. "And also may I be permitted to present myself, as it is a sad necessity that you travel without one from whom I might request the introduction?" he asked of me with a beautiful reverence.

After a search in his pocket for a few seconds he at last discovered a case of leather and presented to me a card. As he handed it to me his color rose up under his black eyes and grave trouble looked from between their long black lashes. I glanced down at the card and read:

Capitaine, le Count Armond de Lasselles,
Paris,
France.
44th Chasseurs de le Republique Francaise.

"Monsieur le Count, I know, I know why it is that you go to America!" I made exclamation as I clasped to my breast my hands and my eyes shone with excitement. "I have read it in *Le Matin* just the day before yesterday. You go to buy grain against the winter of starvation in the Republique. No man is so great a financier as you and so brave a soldier, with your wound not healed from the trenches in the Vosges. Monsieur, I salute you!" and I bent my head and held out my hand to him.

"We're to expect nimble wits as well as courage of you young - shall I say *American* women?" he laughed as he bent over my hand. "Now shall I not be led for introduction to the small brother and the old nurse?" he asked with much friendly interest in his kind eyes.

It was a very wonderful thing to observe the wee Pierre listen to the narration of Capitaine, the Count de Lasselles, concerning the actions of a small boy who had run out of a night of shot and shell into the heart of his regiment and who had now lived five months in the trenches with them. Pierre's small face is all of France and in his heart under his bent chest burns a soul all of France. It is as if in her death, at his birth, my beautiful mother had stamped her race upon him with the greater emphasis.

"Is it that the small Gaston is a daredevil like is my Bob?" he questioned as we all made a laughter at the story of the Count de Lasselles concerning the sortie of the small idol from the trenches in the dead of one peaceful night to return with a very wide thick flannel shirt of one of the *Boches*, which he had caught hanging upon a temporary laundry line back of the German trenches.

At that English "daredevil" word I was in my mind again back in the old Chateau de Grez and into my own childhood.

"You young daredevil, you, hold tight to that vine until I get a grip on your wrist, or you'll dash us both on the rocks below," was the exact sentence with which my father bestowed my title upon me as he hung by his heels out of a window of the old vine-covered Chateau de Grez.

"It is one large mistake that my *jeune fille* is born what you call a boy in heart. *Helas!*" sobbed my beautiful young French mother as she regarded us from the garden below.

"If you were a boy I'd thrash you within an inch of your life, but as you are a girl I suppose it is permissible for me to admire your pluck, Mademoiselle Roberta," said my father as he landed me in the music room by his side while an exchange of excited sentences went on between my mother and old Nannette in the garden below. "What were you doing out on that ledge, anyway? It is more than a hundred feet to the ground and the rocks."

"I was making the hunt through Yellowstone Park that you have related to me, father, and I prefer that you give me a boy's punishment. If I have a boy's what you call 'pluck,' I should have a boy's what you call 'thrashing.' Monsieur, I make that demand. I am the Marquise de Grez and Bye, and it may be that as you are an American you do not understand fully the honor of the house of Grez." I can remember that as I spoke I drew my ten-year old body up to its full height, which must have been over that of twelve years, and looked my father straight in the face with a glance of extreme hauteur as near as was possible to that of the portrait of the old Marquis de Grez, who died fighting on the field of Flanders.

"*Eh, la la*, what is it I have produced for you, Henri of America? It is not a proper *jeune fille*, nor do I know what punishment to impose upon her; but with you I must laugh," with which my beautiful mother from the doorway threw herself into the arms of her young American husband and her laughter of silver mingled with his deep laugh of a great joy.

"Don't worry, Celeste; Bob is just a clear throw-back to her great-grandmother, Nancy Donaldson, who shot two Indians and a bear in defense of her kiddies one afternoon while my maternal grandsire was in the stockades presiding over the council in which was laid down the first broad draft for the formation of the Commonwealth of Harpeth. I'm sorry, dear, that she is so vigorously American that she has to climb the Rocky Mountains even here in the garden spot of France. Just now she is French enough to be dealing with me in the terms of that jolly old boy of Flanders fame in the hall downstairs; but cheer up, sweetheart, she's a wild, daredevil American and I'm going to send her back to the plains as soon as she speaks her native tongue with less French accent. Then the rest of us can be happily French forever after."

"I will speak as you do, my father, from this moment forth," I answered him with something that was wild and fierce and free rising in my child's heart. "I will not be a *grande dame* of France. I am a woman of America. I speak only United States." And I clung to my father's arm as he drew me to him and embraced both my laughing mother and me, before I was delivered to old Nannette who, with affectionate French grumblings, led me away to the nursery for repairs.

The scene had become fixed in my memory, for from it had sprung a friendship of a great closeness with my wonderful American father whom love had chained in France. When he rode the great hunter that had come across to him from a friend in Kentucky I demanded to cling behind him or to sit the saddle in front of him, even at times running at his side as long as my breath held out, to rise on his stirrup, like the great terrifying Scotchmen do in battles, and cling as Kentuck made flight over wall or fence. My very slim and strong hands could not be kept from the steering wheel of his long blue racing car, and I could bring down a hare out of the field with any gun he possessed as unerringly as could he. I lived his life with him hour by hour, learned to think as he thought, to speak his easy transatlantic speech, and did equal trencher duty with him at all times, so that muscle and brawn were packed on my tall, broad woman's body with the same compactness as it was packed upon his, by the time I had reached my twenty-first birthday. By that time he and I had been alone together for eight long years, for my mother had left us with tiny, misshapen Pierre as a heart burden but with only each other to be companions.

The efforts of some of my mother's distant relatives and friends to make me into the traditional young French Marquise had resulted in giving to me a very beautiful *grande dame* manner to use when I stood in need of it, which I took a care was not too often. Because I had been born to a woman's estate I considered I must manage well beautiful skirts and lacy fans, but no oftener than was necessary, I decided. I went for the most of my days habited in English knickerbockers under short corduroy skirts, worn with a many-pocketed hunting blouse. On the night of my presentation at the salon of my distant relative, the old Countess de Rochampierre, I had to apologize to a young Russian attache for searching with desperation for the bit of lace called a handkerchief, among the laces and ruffles of my evening gown in the regions where I had been accustomed to find sensible pockets.

"And is it possible that Mademoiselle Americaine hunts as well as she makes the dance?" was his delighted answer to my explanation, which led into a half-hour description of a raw morning in the field just three days before in England, where my father and I had gone over for a week's hunting with Lord Gordon Leigh at Leigholm.

"And then some," I returned answer with delight at his sympathy in my narration of the sport. I liked very well the American slang that my father's friends were always glad to teach to me, and that gave to him both amusement and delight when I used it in his presence.

Also I liked well that young Russian and he came many times to the Chateau de Grez and Bye before he left to join his regiment of Russian Cossacks in the Carpathians.

And this time it was from the Carpathians that I returned to the ship deck to find wee Pierre laughing again over the very small dog that brought into the French trenches a very large and stupid sheep from the flock back of the German trenches.

"And your medal of honor, Monsieur le Capitaine; is it permitted that I lay for a little moment just one finger upon it?" Pierre asked of him as the great soldier stood tall above the steamer chair and gave to the little Frenchman the salute of an officer.

Nannette sobbed into her lace and I turned my head away as the tall man bent and laid the frail little hand against his decoration which he wore almost entirely hidden under the pocket of his tweed Norfolk of English manufacture. Only French eyes like wee Pierre's could have seen it pinned there hidden over his heart. I think he wore it to give him a large courage for his mission that meant bread or starvation to so many of his people.

"Ah, Monsieur le Capitaine," I said to him with a softness of tears in my throat, "I would that there was some little thing that I might do to serve France. I do so long to go into those awful trenches with that red cross on my arm, as it is not permitted to me to carry a gun, which I can use much better than many men now handling them with bullets against the enemy; but it is necessary that I obey the commands of my soldier father and take to a safety the small Pierre." And as we spoke he walked beside me to the prow of the large ship so that to us was a view of the heavens of blue beyond which lay our America.

"My child, there is a great service which you can render France," he answered me as we stopped to watch the great white waves flung aside from the ship. "France needs friends in America, great powerful friends who will help her in contracting for food and all other munitions. A beautiful woman can do much in winning those friends. You go to your uncle, who is one of those in power in a State in that fruitful valley of the Mississippi from which I hope that my lieutenant, Count de Bourdon, whom I sent on that mission, will get many mules to carry food to the hungry boys in the trenches when mud is too deep for gasoline. Make of him and everyone your friend and through you the friend of our struggling country. Tell them of France, laugh with them for the joy to come when France, all France, with Alsace and beautiful Lorraine, is free; and make them weep with you for her struggles. Who knows but that through you may come some wonderful strength added to your old country from the new, whose blood runs in your veins as well?"

" All of that I will do, *mon Capitaine*. I so enlist

myself." And as I spoke I drew myself up unto the greatest height possible to me. "I will be of the army that feeds, rather than of that which kills."

"*Mon Dieu*, child, what is possible to you to do has no limit. Also, I say to you, watch and be on your guard for aught that may harm France. In America are spies. I have been warned. Also there are those who practice deceptions in contracts. It is for the purpose to so guard that I come to America."

"I also will so guard," I made answer to my Capitaine, the Count de Lasselles, as we again came in our walk to the side of wee Pierre and old Nannette.

Maria Thompson Daviess

CHAPTER II

VIVE LA FRANCE

And after that first day there were many hours that the Capitaine, the Count de Lasselles, spent with little Pierre and the good Nannette, as she sat knitting always with the sun on the water reddening her round cheeks, while I had much pleasure with many friends who came to me upon the ship.

A very fine young man who was named William Raines, from the State of Saint Louis, instructed me in several beautiful dances, but I do not think he was held in the esteem which he deserved by another of his American brothers by the name of Peter Scudder, whose home was in the town of Philadelphia.

"Dancing with Scudder must be like going to your grandmother's funeral over the old State Road in a rockaway," was the comment that Mr. William Raines made upon his friend Mr.

Peter Scudder, and what Mr. Scudder said of him was of the same unkindness.

"Raines' dancing is extremely like Saint Louis: delightfully rapid but crude," was his comment.

I should have been regretful of the unkindness between those two very nice Americans but for a beautiful good to France that was brought about by the desire of each to please me more than the other.

The many ladies upon the ship had been of exceeding kindness to me because of the loveliness of small Pierre's dark face and the pity of his crooked back. Old Nannette was of a very great popularity with all of those ladies and she spent many hours in recounting the glories of the old Chateau de Grez and Bye and the family which had inhabited it since the fourteenth century. So it came about that many friends were made for France among them.

Now that Mr. William Raines had a very nice idea to invite in my honor all of the ladies who were friends to me, and many distinguished gentlemen of politics and of universities and other large affairs, who were returning from business in Europe to more business in America, to be present while a young boy of France, who was among those in the steerage going to the freedom of America with his mother who had been widowed at Ypres, sang in a very lovely voice many French folk songs and songs of war to all present. And at that singing many tears flowed and so much money was put into the hands of the boy that a future for the very sad little French family was assured in America. And I also wept. I was taken into the embrace of all of those kind American women and assured of so much care and affection in that land of my father, that I felt of a very great richness in spite of the small sum of money in the heel of Nannette's rough stocking. And as I received all of these beautiful attentions I perceived the eyes of my Capitaine, the Count de Lasselles, fixed upon me with a deep gratitude and pride. It was all of a

Maria Thompson Daviess

great pleasure to me except that I did not like very well to be so distinguished by a young man, which made the French *grande dame* in me to shrink.

"*Mais, vive la France,*" I murmured to myself and was happy again.

But, alas! At the joy of all this entertainment there was one sadness. It was of my dear friend, Mr. Peter Scudder. There was no pleasure, but great seriousness, in his face during the whole afternoon.

"Don't mind him; poor Pete's chewing a grouch," was what his good friend Mr. William Raines answered to my lament over his sadness. And that sadness lasted for three days, up unto the day before we came to a sight of the Lady of Liberty of America. Then his face found a great radiance and I perceived that he was full of much business. I found him with a notebook, in deep consultation with my Capitaine, the Count de Lasselles, and then in earnest consultation with many of the other gentlemen. I had much wonder; but at the dinner that night, which was the last before we made the landing to America, I discovered all of his good actions. While we were at the last of the coffee, Mr. Peter Scudder arose and made a bow to the capitaine of the ship, beside whom I sat, which salutation did not in any way include me, and then turned to the direction of my Capitaine, the Count de Lasselles.

"Sir," he said in that very nice voice which it is said is of Philadelphia, "I have the honor to ask you if you will take charge of a fund of five thousand dollars, which has been given by the passengers of this boat, to be sent immediately to a field hospital of France, preferably the nearest in need to the battlefield of the

Marne." And with no more of a speech than that he seated himself and did not so much as make a glance in my direction when he mentioned the battlefield on which my father had died. I think that Mr. Peter Scudder is a very great gentleman and I sat very still and white, with my head held high and tears rising from the depths of France in my heart.

"My honored friends," answered my Capitaine, the Count de Lasselles, as he rose from his place at the foot of the table and stood tall and slim in the manner of a great soldier, "it is impossible that I say to you my gratitude for this expression of your friendship for my country. So many dollars will bring life and an end of suffering to many hundreds of my brave boys, but the good will and sympathy it represents from America to France will do still more. The fund shall go to the place you request and I now beg to offer to you a toast that will be of an understanding to you." And at that moment he raised his glass of champagne and said:

"To the destiny of those born of American and French blood commingled!"

All those present arose to their feet and drank that toast with loving looking at me, and I did not know what I should do until that good old gray boat capitaine patted me upon the shoulder and said across his empty glass:

"God bless and keep you, child!"

"I thank everybody," I answered as I went into the embrace of my very large lady friend from the State of Cincinnati, and then into the embrace of the other ladies.

Maria Thompson Daviess

"I've been knitting all day for two months but I'm going to begin to sit up at night," sobbed the lady from a queer Keokuk name as I took her into my embrace on account of her extreme smallness.

It was at a very late hour, just before retiring, that I ascended to the deck with my Capitaine to view the effect of a very young moon on the waves of the ocean.

"Is it that you think now your soldier of France has done your command well, *mon Capitaine?*" I asked of him.

"Most extremely well, and entirely in the mode of a woman. Those two young men have made of themselves very noble competitors for your favor, but remember that it is of a truth that only a 'daredevil' would bring together such high explosives. I salute you!" he made answer to me with a laugh which ended in a sigh. "Child, little child," he continued as he bent over my hand to kiss it as he did each night before he conducted me to the head of the stairs leading down into my cabin, "above all take unto yourself all that is possible of joy in the present, for we do not know what the supply will be for the future. Perhaps it will be like the harvests of France - burned up in a world-conflagration."

"Ah, but, *mon Capitaine*, will you not dance with me once to-night for a joy. It will be our last on the ship before we land to-morrow. You have never danced with me and to-morrow you are lost from me into the wilds of that English Canada." And as I spoke I held out my arms to him and began to hum the music of that remarkable Chin-Chin fox dance that I had been dancing below with Mr. William Raines and which the band had just begun to play again. Of course, I knew that I must be very lovely in that young moonlight in one of the frocks that Nannette had purchased from her very talented cousin, the *couturiere* on Rue Leopold, and I could see no reason why I should not make a happiness for the great gentleman of France as well as the young boy from Philadelphia and also the one from Saint Louis.

"You *are* a daredevil, Mademoiselle, to propose the dance to powder-stained Armond Lasselles, but the joy of you is of a greatness and I feel from it a healing in the night of my soul."

And he reached out in the moonlight and took me into his arms and danced me along that deck with a grace that it would not be possible for either the one from Philadelphia or the one from Saint Louis to imitate. That nice but very ponderous lady from the State of Cincinnati who regarded us from her steamer chair, enjoyed it as much as did I, and she clapped her large hands as Monsieur le Capitaine swung me around into the quietness beyond one of the tall chimneys for smoke from the engine.

"This is good-bye, *mon enfant*, for I leave the ship at dawn with the tug, so that I do avoid those reporters from newspapers and the contract conspirators. I have advised Nannette that you go to the Ritz-Carlton to await your Uncle if he be not upon the dock. I go to the grain fields of Canada and then to the West of America.... I would that it could be *au revoir*. Upon a day that shall come, beautiful lady, perhaps it will be permitted to me to... *Non, vive la France! A lies vite, cherie* ... go while I - I - *Vive la France!*"

Maria Thompson Daviess

And tears came across my eyes as I did his bidding and left him - to France. In my heart was a desire to cling to him in a great fear at being alone to care for the good Nannette and the small Pierre, but I knew he must travel fast and far on his quest and that for France I must let him go without - a backward look. Would I find in the great land of America such another gallant gentleman to care for the fate of the small Pierre and Nannette and me? What did I know of this cruel Uncle? Nothing but his hardness of heart. I dreaded the sight of him that I should find upon the arrival of the ship at the dock, which would be an answer to the letter I had sent to him to inform him of my coming, and I spent my long night in hate of him.

With the arrival of the morning came more mines that exploded for me under the waves of my life that had danced with so little concern through the days upon the ship. A rain was falling and my friend of France was gone from me at the beginning of day in a boat that is called tug. Upon Nannette had fallen a rheumatism and the small Pierre was in the midst of shivering chills when we at last were permitted by the very unpleasant officer of America to go from the ship.

"*Helas*, it was all of the gold that he took from me for an entry into this savage land where one piece of money is as five of that of France. There remains but a few sous and a gold piece," sobbed Nannette as she came from her interview with the immigration officer while I stood beside Pierre, deposited by a deck steward on a pile of our steamer blankets.

"Did it take all - all of the money to land, Nannette? Not all!" I cried as I stretched out my hand to her. I did not know as I now do, that the money would have been returned to Nannette had she waited with patience and not made a hurry of returning to her nurslings.

"All, Mademoiselle," were the words with which she answered me, and for some very long moments I stood dazed and struggled in the waves of that adventure I had thought to be life.

"I beg your pardon, Marquise, but here is a letter the dock steward failed to find you to deliver," came in the pleasant voice of that Mr. William Raines as he raised a very fine hat that made him much better to look upon than the cap of the steamer, and handed me a large letter. I took it and came with my head out from under the wave which had dashed over me.

"Is there anything I can do to help you through the customs?" then came the nice voice of that Mr. Peter Scudder of Philadelphia from the other side of me.

"No, with much gratitude to you both; I must wait the arrival of my Uncle," I made answer to them with my head held very high.

"Then we'll see you at the Ritz for tea at five as per promise," said Mr. William Raines as he walked away and left Mr. Peter Scudder, who was assisting the lady from Cincinnati to transport her very lovely dog to a handsome car which awaited her. She also had I promised to visit from that great Ritz-Carlton hotel and she smiled in sweet friendliness to me as I stood with the letter in my hand and watched all of the friends I had found upon that ship, depart and leave me with not a place to go. I stood for many minutes motionless and then my eyes perceived the letter in my hand. Surely it must be opened and read. It was from the wicked

Uncle, I knew, but it might be that it was not of the cruelty that I had expected. It would excuse him no doubt from arrival in person for the expected greeting to his relatives, Pierre and myself.

"Go to it, Bob," I advised myself in the language I had heard Mr. Saint Louis use when he was forced to ask a nice lady, who danced with disagreeable heaviness, to trot the fox with him because of a friendship with his mother.

And this is the letter that my eyes read with astonishment, while both the good Nannette and small shivering Pierre sat with their eyes fixed upon my countenance:

"My dear nephew Robert:

"Your arrival in America at this time suits me exactly. I need you immediately in my business. If you had been the girl, instead of the little one, I would have had to dispose of you some way - even murder. I have no use for women. Leave the little crippled girl and her nurse, who I feel sure is an old fool, with my good friend Dr. Mason Burns, of 222 South 32nd St. He has cured more children of hip joint disease than any man in the world, and he will straighten her out for us and we can give her away to somebody. I've written him instructions. Leave her immediately and come down here to me on the first train. The deal is held up without you. Enclosed is a check for a thousand dollars. If you are like Henry you'll need it, but keep away from Broadway and the women. Come on, I say, by next train.

Your uncle, Robert Carruthers.
Hayesville, Harpeth."

"The Uncle of America has come to a confusion of the sex between Pierre and me from a careless memory and the writing of my hand, which is of a great boldness, but not to be easily read," I explained as I read the letter aloud to Pierre and Nannette.

It took me just one hour by the clock, sitting there on the pile of steamer wraps with the small Pierre in the hollow of my arm, to explain and translate the sense of that letter to old Nannette, and I feel sure she would have been sitting upon that spot yet immovable rather than let me depart from her if I had not put all of my time and force upon the picturing to her of a Pierre who could come down with her later to me in a condition to run through the gardens of Twin Oaks, which was the home of his American ancestors. With that vision constantly before her she let the porter and me insert her into a taxicab and extract her at the door of the small private hospital of the good Dr. Burns who was to perform the miracle for the back and hip of small and radiant Pierre.

"But what is it that I do to permit the *jeune fille* of my beloved mistress to depart into this city of wicked savages not attended by me? I cannot. Do not demand it!" were the words with which I left her arguing with that very sympathetic and sensible doctor of America. He had not noticed a confusion of sex was between Pierre and me and he had sent out the check of my wicked Uncle and procured the American money for me. Also he had given me a few directions that he appeared to think of a great sufficiency and had ordered a taxi to be in readiness for me.

"Nonsense, Nurse," he said to Nannette bruskly but not with unkindness when I had translated to him

Nannette's weeping protests. "A great strapping girl like that can get down to the Harpeth Valley all right by herself. Nobody's going to eat her up, and from the size of the biceps I detect under that chiffon I think she could give a good account of herself if anybody tried. How like you are to what Henry was at your age, child, God bless you! I'd go to the station with you but I've a patient all prepared for an operation. Shall I send a nurse with you?"

"No, please, good Doctor, and good-bye," I said, with a great haste as I hurriedly embraced both Nannette and the small Pierre and departed down the broad steps into the taxi with the open door.

"Pennsylvania Station! Your train may not leave for hours, but you can get your baggage together. Good-bye," said that good Doctor as he shut the door and returned to his pursuit of making human beings either whole or dead.

"And now, Roberta Carruthers, no longer Marquise of Grez and Bye, you are in your America, and let's see you do some hustling," as remarked that Mr. Saint Louis to Mr. Peter Scudder at cards.

And while that very swift taxi conveyed me to the large station that is as beautiful as a cathedral I did some what I name "tall thinking." What would be the result of my womanly arrival in that State of Harpeth of my wicked Uncle? Would he be forced to murder me as his letter had said? And if in his anger over the mistake he had made from my letter, written in that very bold and difficult handwriting, he should turn from me, and the good Nannette and Pierre as well, what would I then do? All must be enacted that a cure for Pierre be obtained. With great energy I had been thinking, but I did not know what it was that I should do to prevent his anger when I arrived to him as a woman until suddenly the good Doctor Burns' kindness in marking the resemblance of me to my father in his extreme youth made an entry into my brain and was received with the greatest welcome by the daredevil who there resides.

"Very well, Robert Carruthers, who is no longer the beautiful Marquise of Grez and Bye, you will be that husky nephew to your wicked Uncle in the State of Harpeth whom he 'needs in his business.' What is it that you lack of a man's estate save the clothes, which you have money in your pockets to obtain after you have purchased the ticket upon the railway train?"

A decision had been made and action upon it had begun in less than a half hour after the purchase of the ticket for the State of Harpeth had been accomplished.

As my father had taught me observation in hunting, I had remarked a large shop for the clothing of men upon the Sixth Avenue near to the station. I made my way into it and by a very nice fiction of an invalid brother whom I was taking to the South of America I was able to buy for a few dollars less than was in my pocket two most interesting bags of apparel for a handsome young man of fashion. The man who assisted me to buy was very large, with a head only ornamented with a drapery of gray hair around the edges, and he spoke much of what his son deemed suitable to make appearance in the prevailing mode.

"He's at tea at the Ritz-Carlton with a lady friend this afternoon, and I wish you could have saw him when he left the store to meet her," he said as he laid the last of the silk scarfs and hose into one of the large flat bags I had purchased and which he had packed as I selected. "He had on the match to these gray tweeds and was fitted out in lavender from the skin out. Now what are you going to do about shoes, Miss?"

"That I do not know, kind sir," I made answer with a great perplexity. "I think that the feet of my relative are about the size of those I possess."

"Most women would wear shoes near the size of their brothers' if they didn't prefer to waddle and limp along with their feet scrouged. Go over to the shoe department and the clerk will fit you out with what you need in about two sizes larger than you wear. If they are not right you can tell just about what will be, and exchange 'em by special messenger. I'll pack all this shipshape before you come back." With which direction I left the kind man and made my way to another of equal kindness.

"I have had upon my feet the shoes of my brother when in accidents while at hunting and fishing, and I think I can ascertain a good fitting," I made a falsification to the very polite young man who stood with attention and sympathy to wait upon me.

"We'll make a selection and then try one pair on," he advised me.

And as I gave to him a fine description of the clothing I had purchased he brought forth in accord many wonderful boots and shoes for the riding and a walking and also for the dance. I had never observed that the shoes of men were of such an ugliness; but when one was upon my foot, in place of the shoe of much beauty which I discarded, both I and the young man had a fine laugh.

"*Mais*, they are of a great comfort," I further remarked. "And they feel about as did those of my brother, who is of a small frame."

"Well, if they are not right, send 'em back and I'll change 'em," he answered with great interest.

After the exchange of much money between us, the young man went with me to the other kind old man of the white hair, and together they made places in the two bags for the shoes.

"Just seven hundred dollars all told, and the like of that outfit couldn't be bought any other place of style in New York for less than a thousand, Miss," remarked to me the elderly clerk as he closed and made fast with keys the two bags. "Shall I send 'em special?"

"I'll thank you that you call a taxi for me, Monsieur," I answered, and as he had mentioned that Ritz-Carlton Hotel, in conversation earlier, that very wicked dare-devil that resides within me awoke at attention with the large ears of great mischief. I felt in my pocket that there was still much gold, and the man from whom I had purchased the ticket to the State of Harpeth had assured me that the train did not depart until the hour of six in the evening.

"To the Hotel of the Ritz-Carlton," I commanded the man of the taxi as he made fast the door.

It then transpired that one hour from the time that the

young Mademoiselle Grez, who had registered at that large hotel with all of her luggage from the steamer while by lies her father was represented as still engaged with the customs, entered her room, there emerged young Mr. Robert Carruthers, who, after paying his bill in his room had a hall boy send his bags on ahead of him to the Pennsylvania Station while he sauntered into the tea room. I have never again met with the wonderful dresses I left in that hotel room. I hope the poor and beautiful domestic, who assisted me in cutting my hair into a football shortness after the mode of a very beautiful woman dancer which she said girls of much foolishness in America have affected, was rewarded with them.

And as I stood in the center of the great room of conversation and lights and flowers and music I again became the frightened girl upon the dock of America and I felt as if I must flee, but at that exact moment I beheld my Mr. William Raines of Saint Louis and my Mr. Peter Scudder of Philadelphia seated at a table in a very choice corner and there was a vacant chair between them. Upon each other they were glaring and before I had a thought I started towards them to prevent the carnage that had threatened on the boat.

CHAPTER III

THAT MR. G. SLADE OF DETROIT

A number of moments in the rapid passing of the next few months I have wondered what would have resulted if I had taken that vacant chair between very agreeable Mr. William Raines and very proper Mr. Peter Scudder so evidently reserved for the young, beautiful and charming Marquise of Grez and Bye. I have decided that in about the half of one hour young Mr. Robert Carruthers would have been extinct and the desired and beloved Marquise in her place between them sipping her tea while making false excuses for forgiveness. I did not take that seat but I accepted one which a *garcon* offered me next to them and did regard them with both fear and wistfulness, also with an intense attention so that I might acquire as much as possible from them of an American gentleman's manner.

"I suppose the dame's fussing up for us to the limit, Peter," observed that Mr. Saint Louis while he emptied a glass of amber liquid and removed a cherry from its depths with his fingers and devoured it with the greatest relish. "Gee, but the genuine American cocktail is one great drink! Have another, Peter. You're so solemn that I am beginning to believe that *belle Marquise* did put a dent in your old Quaker heart

Maria Thompson Daviess

after all."

"There was something in that girl's eyes as they followed us, William, that no cocktail ever shaken could get out of my mind," made answer the very grave Mr. Peter Scudder of Philadelphia. "Do you suppose her Uncle got there or that anything happened? I wish I had waited with her."

"Well, either Uncle did arrive or we'll see her in the Passing Follies week after next, third from the left, in as little as Comstock allows. When I've had a good look at bare arms my judgment connects mighty easily with bare -"

By that moment I had poised in my hand a very fragile cup of nicely steaming tea and it was a very natural thing that I should hurl its contents in the face of that Mr. William Raines of the country of Saint Louis.

Voila! What happened? Did I stay to fight the duel with that, what I know now to call a cad, and thus be put back into the person of the Marquise de Grez and Bye for a wicked Uncle to murder. I did not. I placed upon the table two large pieces of money and I lost myself in the crowd of persons who had risen and gathered to sympathize with poor Mr. Saint Louis. No one had remarked my escape, I felt sure, as I had been very agile, but as I sauntered out into the entresol of the Hotel of Ritz-Carlton, to which I had given so great a shock in its stately tea room, a finger was laid upon my arm in its gray tweed coat. I turned and discovered a very fine and handsome woman standing beside me and in her hand she had a book of white paper with also a pencil.

"I was sitting just back of Willie Raines and I heard what he was saying about some woman, whom he and Peter Scudder had met on the boat over, not keeping her appointment with them. Peter is of the Philadelphia elect and nobody knows why he consorts with the gay Willie. I saw them come off the boat together this morning and I knew that the whole Scudder Meeting House would be in a glum over their being together. Would you mind telling me just why you soused your tea into his face? It would make a corking story for my morning edition. Did you know them or did you know the lady or did you do it to be launcelotting?"

"I think it must have been for the third of those reasons, Madam, but I am not sure that I know the word you use," I answered with much caution.

"Launcelot, you know, the boy that was always fussing around over injured women, in Tennyson or some-where, just for a love of 'em that was always perfectly proper. Nice of him but not progressive. Say, do you mind sitting down in a quiet corner of the tea room and telling me all about it? Are you French or Russian or Brazilian, and do you believe in women, or is it just because you like 'em that you threw the tea? I've got a suffrage article to do and I believe you'd make a good headline, with your militant tea throwing. Want to tell me all about it?"

"I have just one hour before going to the State of Harpeth, many miles from here, Madam," I made answer with a great politeness. "I thank you but I must make my regrets."

"Oh, I can find out all I want to know about you in five minutes. Just come sit down with me and be a good boy. Do you want to give me your name? I wish you really were *somebody* that had given Willie that tea fight." And while making protestations and remonstrances I was led again into that tea room and seated at a great distance from the table which had been occupied by that Mr. William Raines and Mr. Peter Scudder, who had now departed. "If you really were some big gun it would kill Willie dead."

"Then, Madam, permit me to present myself to you as Robert Carruthers, Marquis de Grez and Bye, from Paris on my way to visit my Uncle, General Robert Carruthers, of the State of Harpeth. I would very willingly by information or a sword kill that Mr. William Raines of Saint Louis and I regret that - that - " At the beginning of my sentence I had drawn myself up into the attitude of the old Marquis of Flanders in the hall of the ruined Chateau de Grez, but when I had got to the point - of, shall I say, my own sword? - I was forced to collapse and I could feel my knees under the tea table begin to shake together and huddle for their accustomed and now missing skirts.

"That's fine and dandy," answered the nice woman as she began to write rapidly upon the blank paper. "If you'd drawn fifty swords on Willie and he had knocked you down with the butt end of his teaspoon I'd have put Willie on the run in my write-up. Willie has handed me several little blows below the belt that I don't like. Pretends not to have met me, when Peter Scudder's own sister, whom I knew at the settlement, introduced him to me; and what he did to Mabel Wright, our cub on weddings - Oh, well, Mabel is another story. Now - that copy is ready to turn in when I pad it. I wonder if I will get a favor from the manager or be turned out of the tea room permanently for reporting a fight as aristocratic as this in the sacred halls of the Ritz-Carlton. I'd bet my shoe lacings that fifty people come here every afternoon for a week hoping it will happen again."

"I do like this America, whose movement is so rapid," I made remark as I set down my second cup of tea for the afternoon, this one emptied into my depths instead of the face of Mr. Saint Louis.

"That's good, too," returned my new-found friend with a laugh as she again wrote a word or two on the nice white paper. Then she placed her elbow upon the table, leaned her very firm cheek on her hand, and regarded me with fine and honest and sympathetic eyes. "I wonder what America is going to do to a beautiful boy like you. I'm glad that you are going to beat it to the tall timbers of the Harpeth Valley. There are women in New York who would eat you up alive. There's La Frigeda, alias Maggie Sullivan from Milwaukee, over there devouring you with her eyes at this moment, and that pretty little Stuyvesant Blaine debutante hasn't taken her eyes off of you long enough to eat her spiced ice. I know 'em both and could land something from either one if I introduced you in your title and very beautiful clothes."

"Oh, I beg a pardon of you that I have not the time to have an introduction to your friends," I exclaimed with a very true regret, because I did like that very nice woman and would have liked much to have brought advantage to her. "In less than an hour I must 'beat' to those 'tall timbers of Harpeth' you mention."

"Speaking of the State of Harpeth, I don't know as you'll be so safe after all, young friend, if that is any

Maria Thompson Daviess

sample of the variety of women that flower in that classic land of the cotton and the magnolia which I met at Mrs. Creed Payne's war baby tea the other afternoon," mused my fine friend as I paid the *garcon* for the very good tea. "She is in high-up political circles down there in Old Harpeth and from the bunch of women she was with I make a guess she is taking an interest in war contracts. She was with that Mrs. Benton, who pulled off that spectacular deal for desiccated soups for Greece the other day. My stomach is too delicate to feed soldiers dried dog and rotten cabbage melted down into glue in a can, but they may like the idea if not the soup. Anyway, the woman was a beauty, so don't you let her get you."

"I do not entirely understand you, my dear Madam, and I wish that I might have many days to talk with you about these American customs," I said as I put into my pocket the exchange money handed to me by the *garcon.*

"Well, it is not exactly an American custom I have been putting you next to, and I guess I'm patriotically glad that you don't entirely understand. Now, I'm going to put you on the train for Old Harpeth and kiss you good-bye for your mother. I'm not trusting Frigeda, and she's lingering. Come on if your train leaves at six o'clock."

And while she spoke, my interesting and fine woman rose and allowed me to assist her into her gray coat of tweed that was very like to mine.

It was with regret that I parted from that lady at the door of the taxicab that had been called for her, and I bent over and kissed her hand, the first woman that Mr.

Robert Carruthers had ever so saluted.

"Good-bye, boy! Remember, the tall timbers of Harpeth are best. Run right down and get a Southern belle and beauty to settle down and have a dozen babies for you, just like 'befo' the war.' Good-bye! I'll send you down a paper to-morrow. I don't suppose the New York journals ever penetrate the Harpeth Valley. Good-bye again." And then my friend was gone, leaving me once more alone in New York and very shy of those tweed trousers, which I immediately put with me into another taxicab which was directed to the Pennsylvania Station.

At that Pennsylvania Station I remembered to send to my wicked Uncle an announcement by telegram of my arrival to him and then I got upon the train just in time for its departure.

I have remarked that life is like high waves of fate that break in sparkling white crests over buried mines, and I am now led to believe that many of those mines are but the habitation of mermaids of much mischief. Are all ripples on life due to women at the bottom of the matter? I do not know, but it would seem true from the things that immediately began to befall me. And was it not I, a woman who was called daredevil, who began it all?

These Pullman cars of America in which to travel great distances, are very remarkable for their many strange adventures, and I was very much interested but also perturbed when the black *garcon* placed my bag and overcoat upon the floor at the feet of a very prim lady and left me to stand uncomfortably in the aisle before her.

"Your seat, sir, upper five," he said, and departed with my fifty centimes, which is called a dime in America.

In the little division which I could see was marked five were two nice seats that were to each other face to face, but it appeared that neither of them was vacant for Mr. Robert Carruthers. On one the lady sat with very stiff black silk skirts projecting from her sides, as did her thin elbows also in the stiffness of white linen. Beside her, occupying the rest of her seat, was a hat with large black bows of equal stiffness with the rest of the lady's apparel and disposition not to be friendly. On the seat opposite, which from the nature of my ticket and the case I should have supposed belonged to me, were piled two large bundles, a shiny black bag, a black silk coat, also stiff like the lady, an umbrella, two magazines and a basket of fruit. No place was apparent for me or my bags or my overcoat. It seemed as if it would be best for me to stand in the middle of the car all the way to the State of Harpeth so that the lady's stiffness be not disarranged. I did not know what I should do, and my knees began again to feel weak in that gray tweed and to be cold for their accustomed skirts, but the lady looked out of the window and said not a single word. I did not have any convenient cup of tea in my hand to throw in that lady's face in a manner that would not be permitted a gentleman, but if I had had the very lovely lorgnette that has descended to me from my Great Grandmamma, the wife of the old Flanders grandsire, I would have settled the matter with very little trouble in an entirely ladylike manner. As it was, I did not know what to do but stand and then stand longer. Just at the moment when I began to feel that I would either be forced to forget that I was a gentleman or to faint as a lady, a very nice man touched me on the elbow and said:

"Just drop your bag on her feet and come into the smoker. She's got your game beat," and he passed on down the aisle of that car. I acted upon that very kind advice and I am glad that from the weight of the bag I got at least a small action from the stiff lady if only a groan and a glare. Also I should have been grateful that she had so discourteously treated me so that I was fortunate to receive the attention of Mr. George Slade of Detroit as my first experience in American manhood.

That Mr. Slade of Detroit is a man of remarkable adventures, and he related to me many of them as he sat with me in the place reserved for the smoking of gentlemen. They were all about ladies who resided in the different towns to which he traveled in the pursuit of selling cigars, and he called them all by the name of "skirts."

"I tell you, Mr. Dago, there is a skirt in Louisville, Kentucky, that is such a peach that you'd call for the cream jug on sight. It would pay you to stop off and see her. She's on the level all right, but any friend that took a line from me would be nuts to her. See?" And he bestowed upon me a pleasant wink from his eye. To that I made no response. I could make none.

"Now, Mr. Robert Carruthers," I had said to myself at the beginning of the first story of "skirts," "you will find yourself obliged to be in the presence of men as one of their kind and not throw scalding tea in their faces when they speak of ladies. You are of a great ignorance about the brute that is known as man and you must learn to know him as you do the wild hog in hunting." But even for the sake of a larger education I could not remain, and I fled from that Mr. Slade of

Detroit in one half hour back to the arms of the stiff lady. But when I arrived there I found she had had me removed from her as far as possible to the other end of the car, where I found my bags deposited beside one marked "G. Slade, Detroit."

"Took the liberty of transferring you here above the other gentleman, sir. The lady is nervous," said the conductor of the car as he handed me another ticket.

"Right, old top," said that Mr. G. Slade as he stood beside us, having followed. "If you don't enjoy sleeping rock-a-bye-baby we can put our togs up and you can bunk in with me. I'm not nervous." And with a glance at the very stiff black silk back in the front of the car he made a laugh that I could not prevent myself from sharing. It is then that the delicacy of a woman is so easily corrupted?

"I beg your pardon, conductor, but upper nine is engaged for my son who is to get on at Philadelphia. I must have him just opposite my daughter and me. We are nervous." And as the large and pathetic lady across the aisle from number nine spoke in a most timid voice, that Mr. G. Slade gave one glance at the daughter of whom she spoke, who also must have weighed a great many litre, or what you call in America, pounds, and fled back to the smoking apartment.

It was a very funny sight to behold that small conductor stand with my large bags and overcoat and look around at that car full of ladies for a place in which to deposit me and them, which was not previously occupied by some female of great nervousness.

"Madam, I will have to use the upper of this section," he finally turned and said to the occupant of the number of seven with a very fine determination.

"Certainly, conductor; let me remove my hat and coat," came back the answer in a voice of very great sweetness as the conductor deposited me and my bags down in front of the most beautiful lady in all America, I am sure.

"Thank you for much graciousness, Madam," I said, keeping those gray tweed knees straight out in front of me and very still to prevent trembling.

"Not at all, sir; I only bought the lower half of this section. I am not at all *nervous*," and I could see her mouth that was curled like the petals of an opening rose tremble from a mischief as she regarded the stiff black silk back in the front of the car and the two huge females on our right whose son and brother was to arrive in Philadelphia for their protection.

An equally gay mischief rose in my eyes and responded to that in hers as I responded also by word:

"For which also let us be in gratitude."

Many times in the months that followed have I thought of the lure of the laughing mischief in those eyes that were like beautiful blue flowers set in crystal, and how they were to lead me on into the strange land of men in search of those forbidden fruits. They were the first to offer me affection, excepting perhaps my fine reporter woman with the paper and pencil.

And from that moment on I did very much enjoy

myself in conversation with that Madam Mischief, while we together did watch the retirement of all of the persons in the train. She had many funny remarks to make and made me merry with them so that the hour of eleven o'clock had arrived before we had summoned the very black male chamber-maid to turn our seats into beds. All others were in sleep that was a confusion of sound from everywhere and we must stand in the aisle while the beds were being abstracted.

"Shall I take your bag into the dressing room, sah?" said the black male chamber-maid as if to intimate that I should leave the aisle free for his operations.

"Many thanks, yes," I answered him. "Good night, Madam, and to you again much gratitude for the happiness of an evening," and with all sincerity I directed Mr. Robert Carruthers to bend over her very white hand and kiss it with much fervor that was resulted from the loneliness of the poor Marquise of Grez and Bye, who was but a girl in a strange and large land, although habited in trousers and coat.

"You are a dear boy," she made answer to me with an equal affection as she disappeared into the curtains of her small room. Then I departed to that room reserved for the disrobing of gentlemen. It was without occupation and I opened my large bag and procured the very beautiful silk night robing that the kind man had sold to me that afternoon. It was in two pieces that very much resembled the costume in which gentlemen play tennis, only more ornamented by silk embroidery and braid and buttons. I was regarding them with joy when into the small room came that Mr. G. Slade of Detroit. He was appareled in garments of the same cut only of a very wide red stripe, his hair was very much in confusion and he had a bottle in his hand in which was a liquid the color of cognac.

"I've only been awake for two hours listening to that peach of a skirt trying to make you fuss her a bit, and I thought I would bring you a nip to pick you up after your fight. Gee, it is as I suspected. You are off on a wedding tango and that makes you cold to all wiles! My son, for a wedding garment that thing you have in your hand is a winner. I can't sleep in silk myself because it makes me feel like a wet dog, but you'll be so beautiful in them that the bride will be jealous of you and say that even if you are so pretty now you will fade early or that you buy your complexion at the corner emporium. Go on, put 'em on, or was you just looking at 'em for pleasure and going to save 'em by sleeping 'as is'? Me, I always undress to the skin, but some don't."

"I - I was just looking at them with pleasure," I made haste to answer that Mr. G. Slade of Detroit. "When upon travels I always fear to disrobe myself. I think that I will now retire," and with a haste that made my hands tremble I replaced the sleeping garments in the large bag and prepared to flee down the aisle to the sleeping apartment in which was the protection of another woman's presence.

"Not even a nip before you go?" he asked me as he held the large bottle to his lips and threw back his head for a gurgling down his throat.

"No, with much gratitude, and good night," I answered as I rapidly departed with my cheeks in a flame of scarlet and a fear in my heart. In my flight I passed by that number of seven and came very near opening the curtains of the number of five and precipitating myself upon the bayonets of black taffeta that stood firm from a hat so placed as to bar my intrusion. From that accident I turned and sought the kind black male chamber-maid with a request that he show me how to insert myself into the right place for sleeping.

"Right here, Boss. Climb up on these little steps and then hand me down your shoes. Soft now; I think the lady am asleep."

"Good night, and I'm not nervous," I heard a laugh of mischief come from behind a second and short green curtain, that veils the lower of the sleeping shelves, just as I fell onto my shelf above and lay with a panting of relief.

CHAPTER IV

THE IMPOSSIBLE UNCLE ROBERT

"Robert," I made remark to myself after I had with difficulty removed the tweed coat and the tweed trousers and neatly folded them against ugly wrinkles of to-morrow, "you must become a sport and not climb down there and tell that other woman the truth of your lady's estate and ask her to comfort you with affection. You were born a daredevil and you must remember those two Indians and a bear that the Grandmamma Madam Donaldson murdered for safety for herself and her children. That Mr. G. Slade is just one bear and he's not as dangerous to you as if you wore 'skirts' anyway. And, also, if you are brave and propitiate the wicked Uncle, in just a few months you can travel to where the lovely lady with the blue flower eyes resides, of whom in the morning you must get the address of home, and can then make confession to her and know the joy of having her sisterly embraces that seem of so much sweetness to you now.

"But suppose it is that she arises in the night and leaves the train for her home!" I said to myself as I suddenly sat up in the dark and precipitated my head against the roof of the sleeping shelf.

" I will call down to her and ask the one simple

Maria Thompson Daviess

question," I made answer to myself. Then I reached down my head over the edge of my shelf and called very softly:

"Madam?"

"Yes?" came a soft question in answer and I felt that she arose and brought her beautiful head which had the odor of violets in the waves so heavy and black, up very near to mine. I could feel a comfort from her breath on my cheek.

"I am in fear, Madam, that you should leave the train before I am awake," I said in a voice under my breath. "I do not want that I lose you into this great America."

"Oh, I'm not easily lost."

"I am desolated with loneliness and I must know where it is that you leave the train, immediately, so that I may sleep."

"At Hayesville, Harpeth, you ridiculous boy. Now don't disturb me again. Go to sleep."

As I sank back on my pillow, happy with a great relief, I thought I heard two laughs in the darkness, one in a tone of silver from beneath me and one of the sound of a choke from opposite me where was reposed that Mr. G. Slade of Detroit.

"It is a good chance for you, Robert, that you go to sleep your first night in America with the sound of a nice laugh from two persons of kindness towards you, one of whom is to be with you for a friend in the same - what was it the gray lady with the pencil and paper called it? - 'tall timbers of Old Harpeth' where all is of such strangeness to you." And with this remark to myself I fell asleep, "as is," I think it was that Mr. G. Slade of Detroit called my state of not being disrobed further than trousers and coat.

After many months in which came to me cruel pain and a long hard fight for the honor of my beloved, I cannot but remember that feeling of gratitude that came over me as I went into sleep on that narrow shelf under which lay the beauty of that Madam Patricia Whitworth.

In the eight years that I had become all of life to my father we had made many travels into distant lands and had seen all of beauty that the Old World had to offer seekers after it, but nowhere had I seen the majestic wonder of this, his own land, that I beheld pass by like a series of great pictures wrought by a master. All of the morning I could but sit and gaze with eyes that sometimes dimmed with tears for him as faster and faster I was carried down into his own land of the Valley of Harpeth, which he had given up for love of my Mother and from the cruelness of my wicked Uncle who would not welcome her to his home. When the great Harpeth hills, in their spring flush from the rosiness of what I afterwards learned was their honey-suckle and laurel, shot with the iridescent fire of the pale yellow and green and purple of redbud and dogwood and maple leaf, all veiled in a creamy mist over their radiance, came into view, as we arrived nearer and nearer to Hayesville my hand went forth and grasped closely the hand of Madam Whitworth. That Mr. G. Slade had left the train before my awakening and I felt relief from the absence of his eyes and could express to the beautiful lady the joy that was in my heart.

"And the small homes in the valley, Madam, with the sheep and cattle and grain and children surrounded, they need never fear the fire of shell and the roar of the cruel guns. This valley is a fold in the garment across the breast of the good God Himself and it has His cherishing. Is it that there will be a home for me in its peace and for the small Pierre and the old and faithful Nannette?"

"A home and - and other things, boy - when you ask for them," she answered me with a very beautiful look of affection that while it pleased me greatly also made for me an unreasonable embarrassment.

"Is it that you think I will obtain the affection of my Uncle, the General Robert Carruthers, Madam Whitworth?" I asked of her with a great wistfulness, for I had told her of his summons to me and she knew already the story of his hardness of heart against my mother.

"The General is a very difficult person," she made answer to me, and I saw that softness of her beautiful mouth become as steel as she spoke of him. "To a woman he is impossible, as I have found to my cost, but all men adore him and follow him madly, so I suppose his attitude towards them is different from his attitude towards women. My husband and I disagree utterly about the General. In fact, the old gentleman and I are at daggers' points just now and I am afraid - afraid that he will make it difficult for you to be - be friends with me as I - I want you to be."

"Neither the General Carruthers nor any man, Madam,

dictates in matters of the heart to the Marquise de - that is, to Robert Carruthers of Grez and Bye, if that is the way I must so name myself now," I answered in the manner of the old Marquis of Flanders, tinged with the *grande dame* manner of the beautiful young Marquise of Grez and Bye whom I had murdered and left in that room of the great hotel of Ritz-Carlton in New York.

"It will be delicious to watch his face as you and I alight from this train together, boy. It will be worth the trouble of this hurried trip to New York to be introduced to a person who disappeared suddenly in a tug boat in the open ocean when he should have landed at the docks with the propriety that would have been expected of him." And as she spoke I could see that something had happened in New York which had brought much irritation to the beautiful Madam Whitworth.

"It would seem that it is one of the customs of these great ships to send out passengers from them in those very funny small tug boats," I remarked as I leaned forward to catch a last fleeting glimpse of a lovely girl standing in the doorway of an ancient farmhouse, giving food to chickens so near the course of the railroad train that it would seem we should disperse them with fright. "I wept when I must see my good friend, Capitaine, the Count de Lasselles, depart from our ship in one of those tug boats. It was a pain in my breast that he must leave me to go into the wildness of Canada."

"Oh, then he went to Canada first?" exclaimed that Madam Whitworth as she leaned back on her seat as if relieved from some form of a great anxiety about the departure of that Capitaine, the Count de Lasselles.

"Is it that you are also a friend of my Capitaine?" I demanded with a great eagerness of pleasure if it should be so.

"Oh, no, no, indeed!" exclaimed the beautiful Madam Whitworth. "I was speaking of my own friend who might have taken a Canadian line instead of the American. She is so careless about instructions. Now look; we are beginning to wind down into the very heart of the Harpeth Valley, and by the time you make very tidy that mop of hair you have on your head and I powder my nose, we will be in Hayesville to face the General in all of his glory. Mind you kiss my hand so he can see you! I want to give him that sensation in payment of a debt I owe him. Now do go and smooth the mop if it takes a pint of water to do it. That New York tailor has turned you out wonderfully, but even those very square English tweeds do not entirely disguise the French cavalier. You're a beautiful boy and the girls in Hayesville will eat you up - if the General ever lets them get a sight of you - which he probably won't. Now go to the mop!"

For many years, since the lonely day just after the death of my mother, when my father took me into the furthest depths of his sad heart and told me of his exile from the place in which he had been born, and about the elder brother who had hated my beautiful mother, who hated all women, I had spent much time erecting in my mind a statue that would be the semblance of that wicked and cruel Uncle. I had taken every disagreeable feature of face and body that I had beheld in another human, or in a picture, or had read of in the tales of that remarkable Mr. Dickens, who could so paint in words a monstrous person to come when the lights are out to haunt the darkness, and had carefully patched them one upon another so as to make them into an ideal of an old Uncle of great wickedness. On that very ship itself I had beheld a man, who came upon the lower deck from the engine, who had but one eye and a great scar where that other eye should have been placed. Immediately my image of the General Robert Carruthers lost one of the wicked eyes I had given him from out the head of the stepfather who did so cruelly stare at the poor young David Copperfield, and became a man with only one eye which still held the malevolence that was hurled at that small David. And with this squat, crooked, evil image of the General Robert Carruthers in my heart I alighted from the train into the City of Hayesville, which is the capital of the great American State of Harpeth. The black man had swung himself off with my bags and that of the beautiful Madam Whitworth, who with me was the last of the passengers to descend from the steps of the car.

"My dear Jeff!" exclaimed my so lovely new friend as she raised her veil for a very seemly kiss from a tall and quite broad gentleman with a very wide hat and long mustachios that dropped far down with want of wax that it is the custom to use for their elevation in France, as I well know from my father's wrathy remarks to his valet if he made a too great use of it upon his. "And this is General Carruthers' nephew who came down on the train with me. My husband, Mr. Carruthers of Grez and Bye!" with which introduction she confronted me with the gentleman.

"Glad to know you, young man; glad to know you," he answered as he took my hand and gave it an embrace of such vigor that I almost made outcry. "There's the General over there looking for you. Come to see us sometime. Come on, Patsy!"

Maria Thompson Daviess

"Good-bye, Mr. Carruthers. I'll see you soon," said the beautiful Madam Whitworth as she held out her hand to me. "Do it now; there comes the General! Quick, kiss my hand!"

I bent and did as she bade me and as I had promised her to do, and as I raised myself she slipped away quickly after her husband with a salutation of great coolness to a person over my shoulder and a "How do you do, General Carruthers" remark as she went.

Instantly I turned and faced the materialization of the ogre it had taken me years to build up into my wicked Uncle. And what did I see?

My eyes looked straight into eyes of the greatest kindness and wisdom I had ever before beheld, and it was with difficulty I restrained myself from flinging myself and my suit of English tweed straight into the strong arms and burying my head on the broad deep chest that confronted me as the huge old gentleman, with as perfect a mop of white hair as is mine of black, rioting over his large head, towered over me.

"You gallivanting young idiot, where did you pick up that dimity?" he demanded of me as he laid a large hand with long strong fingers on my shoulders and gave me a slight shake. "Don't tell me it was over Pat Whitworth you had that ruckus at the Ritz-Carlton day before yesterday!"

"No, Monsieur, it was not," I answered, looking him straight in the eyes and feeling as if I was looking into kind eyes that I had seen close to me forever in the old convent in France, and as I spoke I could not help it that I raised my arm in its covering of a man's tweed and let my woman's fingers grasp one of the long fingers on my shoulder and cling to it as I had done other long fingers just like them that had guided my first footsteps down the sunny garden paths of the old Chateau de Grez.

"I'm your Uncle Robert, sonny, and don't you ever forget that, sir," he answered as he gave me another shake and I could see a longing for the embrace, which I so desired, in his keen eyes that had softened with a veil of mist in the last second. "Lord, I'm glad you're not a woman! And from now on just stop knowing the creatures exist - Pat Whitworth and her kind. None of that tea-throwing in Hayesville, sir! We've got work to do to put out a fire - fire of dishonor and devastation. No time for tea-fighting here. Come on to my car over there; we've no time to waste."

"What is it that you say about that throwing of tea which occurred only the day before yesterday in the City of New York many hundreds of miles from here? How did that knowledge arrive here, my Uncle Robert?" I questioned.

"Associated Press, sir. The greatest power in this America. Associated Press! Full account, you and me, titles and all, printed in this afternoon's paper. Any money left of that thousand?"

"No, my Uncle Robert," I faltered. "It was necessary that I spend -"

"Don't tell me about it. I sent it to you so you could get as much as possible out of your system. The hussies! I've got work for you to do here. Forget 'em! Hop in!" And he motioned me into a very large blue touring car that stood beside the station platform.

"Drive to the Governor's Mansion and don't sprout grass under your wheels," he commanded the black chauffeur. "The Governor's Mansion, private door on Sixth Street."

CHAPTER V

"HERE'S MY BOY, GOVERNOR"

And it was en route to the mansion of the Gouverneur of the State of Harpeth that my Uncle, the General Robert, did enlighten me as to the urgent need of me in his affairs of business.

"It is a question of mules, sir, and of a dishonor to the State that I'm going to prevent if my hot old head is laid low in doing it, as it probably will be if I get into the ruckus with Jefferson Whitworth that now threatens. They have insinuated themselves into the confidence of Governor Faulkner until they have made it well-nigh impossible for him to see the matter except as they put it. They will get his signature to the rental grant of the lands, make a get-away with the money and let the State crash down upon his head when it finds out that he has been led into bringing it and himself into dishonor. Why, damn it, sir, I'd like to have every one of them, especially Jeff Whitworth, at the end of a halter and feed him a raw mule, hoof and ears. I'm probably going to be done to death all alone before the pack of wolves, but I'm going to die hard - for Bill Faulkner, who holds in his hand the honor of his State and my State, I'll die hard!" And he spoke the words with such a fierceness that his white mustache, which was waxed with the propriety of the world, divided like crossed silver swords beneath his straight nose with its thin and trembling nostrils.

"It will be that I can help you protect this honor of the Gouverneur Faulkner and the State of Harpeth, will it not, my Uncle Robert?" I asked with a great anxiety. "If you must fall on the field of honor it will be the glory of Robert Carruthers of Grez and Bye to fall beside you, sir. I am a very good sport, my father has said."

"God bless my soul, how like Henry you are, boy!" exclaimed my Uncle, the General Robert, and he did lay one of his long and very strong arms across my shoulder and give to me the embrace for which I had so longed; but for not enough time for me to yield myself to it. "Henry always wanted to tag 'Brother Bob,' and he too - would - have died - fighting for me - at my side. I've been hard - and when I heard of his death - I wanted you, boy, I wanted you more - Now what do you mean, sir, by making me forget for one moment the fix Bill Faulkner and I are in?" And my Uncle, the General Robert, gave to me a good shake as he extracted his very large white handkerchief and blew upon his nose with such power that the black chauffeur looked around at us and made the car to jump even as he and I had done.

"And those mules that it would be your wish to feed to that Mr. Jeff Whitworth, my Uncle Robert, will you not tell me further about them? In Paris it is said that they are a very good food when made fat after being old or wounded in the army. I have -"

"That will do, sir. If you've had to eat mule in Paris don't tell me about it. My constitution wouldn't stand that, though during our war, just before Vicksburg, I ate - but we won't go into that either. Now this is the situation, as much as a lad from the wilds of Paris could understand it. The French Government wants five thousand mules by the fall of the year, and there are no such mules in the world as this State produces. They are sending a man over here to try to make a deal with the State of Harpeth to purchase the mules from private breeders, graze them on the government lands and deliver them in a lot for shipment the first of August at Savannah. There is no authority on the statute book for the State to make such a deal, but Jeff Whitworth has fixed up a sort of contract, that wouldn't hold water in the courts, by which the Governor of the State, Williamson Faulkner, grants the grazing rights on the State's lands to a private company of which he is to be a member, which, in a way, guarantees the deal. They've made him believe it to be a good financial thing for the State and he can't see that they are going to buy cheap stock, fatten it on a low rate from the State and hand it over to the French Government at a fancy rake-off - and then leave him with the bag to hold when the time for settlement and complaint comes. There is a strong Republican party in this State and they're keeping quiet, but year after next, when Bill Faulkner comes up for re-election, downright illegality will be alleged, and he will be defeated in dishonor and with dishonor to the State. I am his Secretary of State and I'm going to save him if I can. And you are going to help me, sir!" And as he spoke my Uncle, the General Robert, gave to me a distinguished shake of the hand that made my pride to rise in my throat, which gave to my speaking a great huskiness.

" I will help in the rescue of the honor of that

Maria Thompson Daviess

Gouverneur Bill Faulkner, my Uncle Robert, with the last breath in my body, and I will also assist to feed mule to that Mr. Jefferson Whitworth, though not to his beautiful wife whom I do so much admire."

"That's just it; she'll have to eat mule the first one. She's at the Governor day and night with her wiles, and in my mind it's her dimity influence that is making him see things with this slant. They say she put her brand on him in early youth. He's the soul of honor but what chance has a man's soul-honor got when a woman wants to cash it in for a fortune with which to lead a gay life? None! None, sir!" And the countenance of my Uncle, the General Robert, became so fierce that it was difficult to find words to answer.

"Oh, my Uncle Robert, is it that a woman would make a cheat in giving the mule animal of not sufficient strength to carry food to poor boys of France in the trenches when there is too much mud for gasoline!" I exclaimed with a great horror from knowledge given me by my Capitaine, the Count de Lasselles.

"Just exactly what she is trying to do, boy. Let those poor chaps with guns in their hands to defend her civilization as well as theirs, die for want of a supply train hauled by reliable mules when unreliable gasoline fails. That's what women are like." And as he spoke I perceived the depth of dislike that was in the heart of my Uncle, the General Robert, for all of womankind.

"There are some women who would not so comport themselves, my Uncle Robert. I give you my word as one - " Then as I hesitated in terror at the revelation of my woman's estate I had been about to make, my Uncle, the General Robert, made this remark to me:

"Women are like crows, all black; and the exceptional white one only makes the rest look blacker. The only way to stop them in their depredations is to trap them, since the law forbids shooting them." And as he made this judgment of women I forgot for a moment that we discussed that Madam Whitworth, whom it was causing me great pain to discover to be the enemy of France, and I thought of my beautiful mother, whom he had judged without ever having encountered, and a great longing rose in my heart so to comport myself that his heart should learn to trust in me as a man and then discover the honor of woman through me at some future time. I took a resolve that such should be the case and to that end I asked of him:

"How is it that I can serve you in these serious troubles, my Uncle Robert?" And as I asked that question I made also a vow in my heart against that black crow woman.

"Now that's what I'm coming to. The French Government is sending an army expert down here to look over the situation and make the contracts. I can't speak their heathenish tongue or read it, and I want somebody whom I can trust - trust, mind you - to help me talk with him and make any necessary translations. That Whitworth hussy has been translating for us and I don't trust her. Your letter was handed to me in the Governor's private office and both he and I saw what a help it would be to have you here when this Frenchie - who is a Count Something or Other - and his servants and secretaries, what he calls his suite, arrive. By George, sir, we need your advice in eating and drinking them! Do you suppose they'll have intelligence enough to eat the manna of the gods, which is corn pone, and drink the nectar, which is plain whiskey, or will we be expected to furnish them with snails and absinthe?"

At that I laughed a very large laugh and made this answer to the perturbation of my Uncle, the General Robert:

"I will tell you after luncheon, my Uncle Robert, because I have not as yet eaten in this Harpeth country of America."

"All right, we'll talk about it after you've had one of old Kizzie's fried chicken dinners. Here we are at the Mansion. Remember, you know the *whole* situation and are only supposed to know the part that Governor Bill *thinks* is the whole. Look at me, boy!" And as the big car drove up to the curb before a great stone house with tall pillars on guard of its front, he laid both his hands upon my shoulders and turned me towards him with force and no gentleness and then with his keen eyes did he look down into the very soul of me.

"Yes, I see I can trust you, sir. God bless you, boy!" he said after a very long moment of time.

"Yes, my Uncle Robert," I answered him without turning my eyes from his.

"Well, then, here we are. I came to the side door so I wouldn't have to introduce you to any of the boys this morning, for we want to have a talk with the Governor before dinner and I don't dare keep Kizzie waiting. It riles her, and a riled woman burns up things: masters, husbands, cooking or worse. Come on." And as we walked up the broad side steps of that Mansion of the Gouverneur, my Uncle Robert's hand was on my arm and I felt that I was being marched up to the mouth of the gun of Fate and I wished very much I could have been habited in my corduroy or cheviot skirts, no matter how short or narrow they might be. A number of gentlemen sat upon the wide verandah smoking pipes or long cigars under the budding rose vine that trailed from one tall pillar to another, and more stood and talked in groups beside the large front door that opened into the wide hall. At the back of the hall before a closed door stood a very large black man who was very old and bent and who had tufts of white wool of the aspect of a sheep upon his head. He was attired in a long gray coat of a military cut that I afterwards learned was of the late Confederacy, and I soon had much affection for him because of his reminiscences of that war and also because of his affection for my noble father, to whom he had told the same stories' in his early youth.

My Uncle, the General Robert, had not paused to present to me any of the gentlemen with whom he had exchanged jovial greetings, but he stopped beside the old black man and said:

"This is Henry's boy, Robert, Cato. Fine young chap, eh?"

"Yes, sir, Mas' Robert," answered Cato as he peered into my face with the nicest affection in his black eyes set in large spaces of white.

"Like Henry, isn't he?"

"'Fore God, yes, sir!"

"Look after him, Cato. He'll be about considerable."

"Dat I will - Mas' Henry's boy!"

"No lobbying dimity chasing him, Cato!"

"Yes, sir; I understands, sir."

"Is the Governor ready for me?"

"Yes, sir, you's to go right in, Mas' Robert. Mr. Clendenning is with him jest now, but he'll be out in a turkey's call of time. Jest walk in, sir, and you, the young marster," and with a bow that almost allowed that the tails of the long gray coat swept the floor, the old black man opened the door and motioned us into the room of the Gouverneur of the State of Harpeth.

It has been given to me in the very short time of my life to be often in the home of the President of France, to be presented at the court of England with my father, to the Czar at Petrograd and to the old Franz Joseph, as well as to the beloved Albert and Elizabeth in Brussels, where I did go often to play with the young princess, and I do know very well how to manage skirts whether very tight, or very wide with ruffles, in the case of such presentations, but my heart rose very high up and beat so near to the roots of my tongue that it was impossible for me to speak as I was presented, in the traveling tweeds of a young man of American fashion, to the very wonderful and beautiful and fearful Gouverneur Williamson Faulkner of the State of Harpeth.

"Here's my boy, Governor," was all the introduction my Uncle, the General Robert, administered to me, and I stood and looked into the face of him whom afterwards I discovered to be the greatest gentleman in the world, with my heart beating in my throat and yet astir under my woman's breast in the place it had always before resided.

CHAPTER VI

"WE BOTH NEED YOU"

I do not know how it is that I shall find words in which to write down the loveliness of that Gouverneur of Old Harpeth. He was not as tall as my Uncle, the General Robert, and he was slender and lithe as some wild thing in a forest, but the power in the broadness of his shoulders and in the strength of his nervous hands was of a greatness of which to be frightened; that is, I think, of which a man should be frightened but in which a woman would take much glory. His hair was of the tarnished gold of a sunset storm and upon his temples was a curved crest of white that sparkled like the spray of a wave. All of which I must have seen with some kind of inward eyes, for from the moment my eyes lifted themselves from contemplating the carpet in embarrassment over my tweed trousers they were looking into his in a way which at dawn my eyes have gazed into the morning star rising near to me over the little wood at the Chateau de Grez. I did not for many days know whether those eyes were gray or blue or purple, for when I regarded them I forgot to decide, and also they were so deep and shadowed by the blackness of their lashes and brows that such a decision was difficult. At this time I only knew that in them lay the fire of the lightning over Old Harpeth when the storm breaks, the laugh of the very small boy who splashes bare feet in the water with glee, and also a coldness of the stars upon the frost of winter. I was glad that I came across the dark ocean to flee from the cruel guns into a strange land to look into those eyes.

"It is good that you have come, Robert Carruthers, for the General and I both need you," were the words I heard him saying to me in a voice that was as deep and of as much interest as the eyes, and as he spoke those words he took one of my hands in both of his strong ones. "And if you say snails, snails it shall be, if Cato and I have to invade every rose garden in Hayesville and vicinity and stay up all night to catch them."

"I think I shall choose that corn pone and whiskey that my Uncle, the General Robert, has promised to me from one bad tempered cook at the time of my luncheon," I found myself saying with a laugh that answered the bare-footed boy who suddenly looked at me out of the cool eyes.

"I thought I would let him have a try-out with Kizzie before we decided what to feed the savages," also said my Uncle, the General Robert, with a laugh. "Besides, he's one himself and I'll have to go slow and tame him gradually."

"No, he's ours. He's just come back to his own from a strange land, General, and you'll kill the fatted calf or rooster, whichever Kizzie decides, with joy at getting him." And this time the star eyes gave to me the quick sympathy for which I had prayed before the Virgin with the Infant in her arms in the little chapel of the old convent just before we had to flee from the shells, leaving my father to the Sisters to bury after the enemy had come. I think my eyes did tell that tale to his and the tears ached in my throat.

"I know, boy," he said softly and then turned and presented me to the Mr. Clendenning who was arranging papers at a desk beside the window.

I do like with my whole heart that funny Buzz Clendenning, who has the reddest hair, the largest brown speckles on his face and the widest mouth that I have ever beheld. Also, his laugh is even wider than is his mouth and overflows the remainder of his face in ripples of what is called grin. He is not much taller than am I, but of much more powerful build, as is natural, though he did not at that moment recognize the reason thereof.

"Shake hands, boys; don't stand looking at each other like young puppies," said my Uncle, the General Robert, as he clapped his hand on the back of the Mr. Buzz Clendenning. "You don't have to fight it out. Your fathers licked each other week about for twenty years."

"Can't I even ask him to take off his coat once, General?" answered that Mr. Buzz with the grin all over his face and spreading to my countenance as he took my hand in his to administer one of those shakes of which I had had so many since my arrival in America. For a second he looked startled and glanced down at my white hand that he held in his and from it to my eyes that were looking into his with the entire friendliness of my heart. Suddenly I had a great fright of discovery within me and my knees began to again tremble together for their skirts, but before that fright had reached my eyes quite, I had born to me an elder brother in the person of that Buzz Clendenning, and I now know that I can never lose him, even when he knows that -

"I'm no shakes in the duel, Prince, so let's kiss and make up before you get out your sword," he said as he also, as my Uncle, the General Robert, had done, laid an arm across my shoulders in an embrace of affection. It was then I made a discovery in the strange land into which I was penetrating: Men have much sentiment in their hearts that it is impossible for a woman to discover from behind a fan. They keep it entirely for each other as comrades, and I received a large portion of such an affection when that Mr. Buzz Clendenning adopted me in what he thought was my foreign weak-0ness, as a small brother to be protected in his large heart.

"I am very happy to so salute you instead of the duel," I made answer and did immediately put a kiss on his one cheek, expecting that he would return it upon my cheeks, first one and then another, as is the custom of comrades and officers in France.

"Here, help! Don't do that again or I'll call out the police," responded that funny Mr. Buzz Clendenning, as he shook me away from him, while my Uncle, the General Robert, and the great Gouverneur did both indulge in laughter.

"I am abashed and I beg your pardon for offending against the customs of your country. I do remember now that my father did not permit such a salutation from his brother officers, and I will not do so again, Monsieur Buzz Clendenning," I said as my cheeks became crimson with mortification and tears would have come over my eyes had my pride permitted.

Maria Thompson Daviess

"This is what he meant you to do, Buzz, you duffer. I said good-bye to twenty-two of my friends this way the day I set sail from old Heidelberg," and as he spoke, that great and beautiful and exalted Gouverneur Faulkner did bend his head to mine and give to me the correct comrade salute of my own country on first one of my cheeks and then upon the other.

"I thank you, your Excellency," I murmured with gratitude. I wonder what that Russian Count Estzker-witch or Mr. Peter Scudder or Lord Leigholm on those Scotch moors, would have thought to hear Roberta, Marquise of Grez and Bye, express such gratitude for two small pecks upon her cheek delivered in America.

"Yes, sir, it's mighty pretty to look at but I reckon the kid had better stow the habit before he is introduced to Jeff Whitworth and Miles Menefee and the rest of the bunch," said that Mr. Buzz as he left off wiping from his cheek with the back of his hand the kiss I had put there, and administered to me another embrace on my shoulders with his long arm. "Besides, youngster, there are *girls* in Hayesville," he added with a grin that again was reflected on my face without my will and which did entirely take away my anger and embarrassment at his repulse.

"Girls! Girls!" exploded my Uncle, the General Robert. "The female young generally known as girls are about as much use to humanity as a bunch of pin feathers tied with a pink ribbon would be in the place of the household feather duster that the Lord lets them grow into after they reach their years of discretion. Robert has no time to waste with the unfledged. Don't even suggest it to him, Clendenning. And now you can take him around to my house and tell Kizzie to begin filling you both up while I wait for a moment to go over these papers with the Governor. And both of you avoid the female young, for we've work for you; mind you, work and no gallivanting. Now go! Depart!"

"The old boy is a forty-two centimeter gun that fires at the mention of the lovely sex and doesn't stop until the ammunition gives out," said Mr. Buzz Clendenning as he slid into the seat of his slim gray racer beside me and started from the curb on high without a single kick of the engine. "I'd like to wish a nice girl, whom he couldn't shake off, onto him for about a week and watch him squirm along to surrender. Wait until you see Sue Tomlinson get hold of him down on the street some day. He shuts his eyes and just fires away at her while she purrs at him, and it is a sight for the gods. Sue's father died and left her with her invalid mother and not enough money to invite in the auctioneer, but the General took some old accounts of the Doctor's, collected and invested them and made up plenty of money for Sue's grubstake, though he goes around three blocks to get past her. Sue adores him and approaches him from all sides, but has never made a landing yet. Say, you'll like Sue. She is pretty enough to eat, but don't try to bite. It's no use."

"Is it that this lovely Mademoiselle Sue does not like gentlemen save my Uncle, the General Robert?" I asked with great interest. I was glad in my heart that I was soon to see and speak with a nice girl even if it had to be in character of a man.

"Oh, she loves us - all," answered that Mr. Buzz with the greatest gloom. "*All* of us - every blamed son-of-a-gun of us."

"Oh, I comprehend now that it is your wish that she love only you, Mr. Clendenning, and are sad that she does not," I said as I looked at him with much sympathy.

"That is about it, Prince, but don't say I said so. Everybody chases Susan. She even wins an occasional ice cream smile from His Excellency. I bet she'd go up against that august iceberg itself in a try-out for a 'First Lady of the State' badge if Mrs. Pat Whitworth hadn't got the whole woman bunch to believe she has a corner on his ice. Mrs. Pat is some little cornerer, believe me."

"Oh, I did like that Madam Whitworth, and I hope that it will be my pleasure to see her again soon," I said with an ice in my voice as I caught my breath while Mr. Buzz Clendenning drove between two cars and a wagon with not so much as an inch to spare on all three sides of the car. It is as I like to drive when at the wheel, but sitting beside another -

"You'll see her at the Governor's dinner for you Tuesday, if not sooner, and just watch her and the General war dance with each other. He opens his eyes when Mrs. Pat attacks and he imagines he is the whole Harpeth Valley Militia defending His Excellency of Iceland from her wiles. Just watch him!" And this time it was three wagons that we slid between and beyond.

"Why is it that the great Gouverneur Faulkner has such a coldness for ladies?" I asked of that Mr. Buzz. "I did find him to be of such a beautiful kindness."

"He's been too much chased. He's got his fingers crossed on them, they tell me. Just watch him in action at his dinner. He side-steps so gently that they never know it."

"Why is it then that he gives to me this dinner of honor when he so dislikes all - that is, I mean to ask of you why is it that I am so honored by that very great Gouverneur Faulkner of the State of Harpeth?" I asked, and I had a great fright that I had again so nearly betrayed Robert Carruthers to be one of the sex so hated by that noble gentleman, the Gouverneur Faulkner. "I must think of myself as a man in future," I commanded myself.

"Didn't the General tell you about it? It is to introduce you to the flower and chivalry of your native land. Believe me, it will be some dinner dance. The General wanted it to be a stag, but Sue fought to the last trench, which was tears, and he gave in. These days the Governor loses no chance to honor his Secretary of State for - for political reasons," and as he spoke that good Mr. Clendenning looked at the wheel for steering, and I could see that there was deep concern in his eyes.

"Is it that - that trouble of mules, Monsieur Clendenning?" I asked of him softly in a woman's way for administering sympathy for distress but without the masculine discretion that I was to learn swiftly thereafter to employ.

"Don't talk about it, for I don't know how much either of us knows or our chief wants us to know, but Governor Williamson Faulkner is a man of honor and I'd stake my life on that. He's being pushed hard and - Gee! Here we are at the General's and I can smell Kizzie's cream gravy with my mind's nose. I understand that your father was the last Henry Carruthers of five born up in the old mahogany bedstead that the General inhabits between the hours of one and five A.M. Some shack, this of the General's, isn't it? Nothing finer in the State." And as he spoke that Mr. Buzz Clendenning stopped the car before the home of my Uncle, the General Robert, and we alighted from it together.

I do not know how it is that I can put into words the beautiful feeling that rose from the inwardness of me as I stood in front of the home of my fathers in this far-away America. The entire city of Hayesville is a city of old homes, I had noticed as I drove in the gray car so rapidly along with Mr. Buzz Clendenning while he was speaking to me, but no house had been so beautiful as was this one. It was old, with almost the vine-covered age of the Chateau de Grez, but instead of being of gray stone it was of a red brick that was as warm as the embers of an oak fire with the film of ashes crusting upon it. Thus it seemed to be both red and gray beneath the vines that were casting delicate green traceries over its walls. Great white pillars were to the front of it like at the Mansion of the Gouverneur, and many wide windows and doors opened out from it. Two old oak trees which give to it the name of Twin Oaks stood at each side of the old brick walk that led from the tall gate, and as I walked under them I felt that I had from a cruel world come home.

CHAPTER VII

THE GIRL BUNCH

And, if I felt in that manner as I entered the house, I felt it to a still greater degree when I was welcomed by that most lovely old black slave woman of the high temper and good cookery. She opened the door for us herself, though a nice boy the color of a chocolate bonbon stood in waiting to perform that office. She had a spoon in her hand and upon her head was a spotless white turban, as also was an apron of an equal spotlessness tied around her very large waist.

"You, Mas' Robert, you done come home from the heathen land to keep my food waiting jest like yo' father did from the minute I ontied him from my apron string. Come right into the dining room 'fore my gravy curdles and the liver wing I done saved for you gits too brown in the skillet," was all of the introduction or greeting that she gave to me as she waddled along behind Mr. Buzz Clendenning and myself, driving us down the hall and into the dining-room. "Mas' Buzz, how is yo' mother? I 'lowed to git over to see her soon as this ruckus of young Mas' coming home is over. Now, here's the place fer you both and that no 'count boy will bring in yo' dinner proper to you or he'll be skunt alive." With which she departed through a door, from which came an aroma that led to madness of

Maria Thompson Daviess

hunger, and left the bonbon servant to attend us.

"Gee, I hope Kizzie killed by the half dozen last night; if there aren't three chickens apiece you'll be hungry, L'Aiglon," said Mr. Buzz Clendenning with a laugh as he seated himself beside me and unfolded his napkin.

"I wish that you might call me Robert, Mr. Clendenning," I said with a great friendliness as I ate a food that I had not before tasted and that I did so much like that I was tempted to steal some to put in my pocket for fear I would come to believe that I had dreamed it to exist. It is called corn pone and is made of maize, and it will be found in some form at every meal upon my Uncle, the General Robert's, table, good Kizzie assured me as I made her a compliment about it.

"Though the name of that son of our great Napoleon is very dear to me," I added at his quick glance, fearing he might think me offended at what is called a nickname.

"Sure, Bobbie, and you'll forget that I wouldn't let you kiss me, won't you?" he answered as he drew back from the table and lit a cigarette after passing me the case. "Everybody calls me Buzz the Bumble Bee because of a historic encounter of mine with a whole nest of bumblebees right out here in the General's garden. It is a title of heroism and I'd like to have you use it as if we'd been kids together as we were slated to have been. Gee, I bet you could have beat the bees down some. You looked all soft to me when I first saw you but you are so quick and lithe and springy that you must be some steel. What do you weigh out, stripped?"

"Er - er, about one-thirty , " I answered, and I made a

resolve not to blush or show anything of embarrassment, no matter what was to be said to me in my estate of a young gentleman.

And I make this note to myself that it is a great pleasure and interest to sit beside a nice young man with a cigarette in his mouth and one in my hand as if for smoking, which I do not like to do from its bitterness, and converse with him about matters of good sense without having in any way to use that coquetry which breaks into small sections the usual conversation between a man and a woman of enthusiastic youngness.

"I tip at one fifty-two, but I'm an inch and a half taller. Do you run? You're good and deep chested," he further inquired and it was with difficulty that I again controlled the blush.

"I fence and I'm large of lung," I answered quickly.

"Ride?"

"Anything ever foaled," I answered in words I had heard my father use about my horsemanship.

"Don't smoke?"

"Don't like it."

"Golf?"

"Some - wild."

"I play a hurry game myself," he laughed. "Dance?"

"With a greatness of pleasure," I answered.

After that for a time he puffed at his cigarette and I looked around the long dining room that was almost as large as the dining-hall at the Chateau de Grez and which was dark and rich and full of old silver on the sideboard and old portraits on the walls. Finally my Buzz put out the stub of his cigarette in his saucer and looked me keenly in the face as I raised my eyes to his.

"Booze?" he asked quietly.

"No!"

"That's good, old top. Me neither! Say, let's go call on Sue and you can get a nice little initiation into the girl bunch before the General stops you by locking you away from them."

"I wish that I might, but I must unpack my bags and write the letters to small Pierre and my nurse Nannette; also be ready for translations for my Uncle, the General Robert, when he arrives. Will you persuade the lovely Mademoiselle Sue that she save one little dance for me on that evening of Tuesday?" I said as we rose and walked down the long hall towards the wide door under the budding rose vine.

"She'll dead sure give you one - of mine," he answered me with a laugh, "but come along with me now, L'Aiglon. The General won't be home until night. I laid some letters on his desk that will hold him and Governor Bill until sunset. They'll have pie and milk sent in and work it all out together. What's the use of having them to watch the affairs of the State of Harpeth for us if we don't use the time they are on watch in having some joy life? Come on!"

"I go," I made answer with a great pleasure.

Then we descended to the gray car of much speed and did use that speed in turning many streets until we came to another very fine old house, where, I was informed by my Mr. Buzz Clendenning, resides that Mademoiselle Susan of so much loveliness.

And it is of a truth that I discovered that loveliness to be as great as was told to me by her true lover. When I raised my head from the kiss of presentation I gave to her hand I looked into very deep and very wonderful girl eyes that had in their depths tears that were for a sympathy for me, I knew. My heart of an exile beat very high in my own girl's breast that ached for the refuge of her woman's arms, and I must have partly betrayed my yearning to her, for I saw an expression of confused question come into her eyes that looked into mine; then the beautiful thing that had come into my Mr. Buzz Clendenning's eyes for me came also into hers in place of the question. I saw then in those eyes a sister born to the boy Robert Carruthers of a great French strangeness.

"I've been thinking about you all morning, Mr. Carruthers, and hoping Buzz would bring you with him to see me first of all. I wanted to be the first one of the girls to say, 'Welcome home' to you." And as she spoke those words of much tenderness I again bent over her hand in salutation because I could give forth no words from my throat.

"Sue, you are the real sweet thing - and now notice me a bit, will you?" said my fine Mr. Buzz Clendenning with both emotion and a teasing in his voice. "I know I haven't got French manners and don't look like L'Aiglon, but I'm an affectionate rough jewel."

"Please don't mind Buzz, Mr. Carruthers - he just can't help buzzing. Isn't it great about the dance Tuesday night? I fought hard to save you from a horrid long banquet with a lot of solemn men. I ought to be the belle of that ball and you and Buzz will be ungrateful if you neglect me," and as she made these remarks for laughter, I liked still more this new friend.

"You are the good, thoughtful little missionary to the foreigner, Susan. I suppose you wanted to stay at home and tat socks while Bobbie and I dined and wined - not," was the very unappreciative answer that was made to her by that Buzz.

"For always I will be your humble slave, Mademoiselle Susan," was the answer I made into her laughing eyes. "All the evening I will wait in loneliness for the small crumbs of dance that you throw to me."

"That will do, Robert; you don't know how spoiled Susan is and you're making trouble for me. Besides, you haven't seen the baby Belle in war paint yet. Let's go call on her now!" And that Mr. Buzz Clendenning was in a moment ready for making more new friends for me. "Come on, Susan, we can tie Prince Bob on the running board."

"Why, there's Belle at the gate now and - yes - it's Mrs. Whitworth with her. I wonder when she came from New York," said Mademoiselle Susan as we went to meet the guests approaching, I on the one side of her and the Mr. Buzz on the other.

CHAPTER VIII

IN THE DRESS OF MAGNIFICENCE

"The beautiful Madam Whitworth came down upon the same train which I occupied," I said as I remembered to raise from my head my hat by that action on the part of my Mr. Buzz.

"Oh, then you have been presented to L'Aiglon?" said Mr. Buzz to that Madam Whitworth who stood smiling while I was presented to the very lovely girl of great blondness, who both blushed and what is called giggled as I kissed her hand, though in her eyes I found a nice friendliness to me.

"We are old friends who know all about each other, aren't we, Mr. Robert Carruthers?" and in her gay answer to that Mr. Buzz I detected a challenge as her eyes of blue flowers in snow looked into mine with the keenness of a knife, to detect if I had yet been told aught of her by my Uncle. And in the answering look of friendliness I gave her was concealed also a knife of great keenness, which came from a brain with which I hoped to do to the death that enemy of France. And also I felt my heart spring to the protection of the honor of great Gouverneur Faulkner, who had given me a comrade's salute within a few hours past; and also to the protection of the honor of my house in the

Maria Thompson Daviess

person of my Uncle, the General Robert.

"Indeed, I have much joy that I was given the opportunity to know the very beautiful Madam Whitworth at so early a time in my life in America," I made answer to her question in words as I bent also over her hand for a kiss of salutation.

And then I had a great amusement at the skill with which that Madam Whitworth brought it to pass that I walked with her from that gate and left the three new and lovely friends I had made looking after me with affection and regret at my departure.

"Of course, it was horrid of me to snatch you like that from those infants, but - I really had the claim to have you for a little time to hear your impressions of Hayesville, now, didn't I? - you boy with eyes as beautiful as a girl's!" she said to me as I walked down the wide street beside her.

"I hope you will always make such claims of me, Madam," I made answer with the great sweetness with which I was determined for the time to keep covered the steel knife.

"I know how to claim - and also to reward," she answered me with a warmth that gave me a great discomfort. "And how did you escape from the General into feminine society on your very first day? Wasn't there work for you at the Capitol? I understand that they are expecting that French Commissioner very soon now." She asked the question with an indifference that I knew to be false.

"I think it is that I am allowed to get my - what you say

in English? - land legs," I answered with much unconcern.

"Speaking of that Frenchman who is coming down for the mule contracts, of which by this time you have doubtless heard, I wonder why it is that the Count of Lasselles, your friend, is sending one of his lieutenants instead of coming himself. Did he say anything of coming down later? I wish he would, for to my mind he is one of your greatest soldiers and I would like to look into his face. That portrait in the *Review* is one of the most interesting I have almost ever seen. Is there any chance of his coming down?" And I was of a great curiosity at the anxiety in her face about the movements of my Capitaine, the Count de Lasselles.

"He told me only that he would go to the grain fields of English Canada, Madam," I answered her by guardedly telling her no more than my words upon that train had revealed to her.

"If he writes to you, you must tell me about it," she said with great friendliness. "I am interested in everything that happens to him."

"I will do that, with thanks for your interest," I answered to her with an air of great devotion. "And behold, is it not the Twin Oaks of my Uncle I see across the street?" I asked as I stopped in front of that fine old home that was now mine.

"Come on down the street to my home and I'll give you a cup of tea," she invited me with very evident desire for my company for more questioning.

"I give many thanks, but that is not possible to me, as I

must write notes to my Pierre and old Nannette for the evening railroad. I bid you good day, beautiful Madam," and again I bent over her hand in a salutation of departure.

"Then I'll see you again soon," she said and smiled at me as I stood with my hat in my hand as she went away from me down the street.

"*Vive la France* and Harpeth America!" I said to myself as I ascended the steps, was admitted by the Bonbon and conducted up the stairway to my apartments by good Kizzie, whom I met in the wide hall.

And there ensued an hour of the greatest interest to me as the very good old slave woman led me from one of the rooms in the large house to another, with many stories of great interest. At last we came to that room in which had been deposited my bags and my other equipment for my journey and there we made a very long pause.

"This is your Grandma Carruthers' room, the General's grandma, and she was the high-headedest lady of the whole family. That am her portrait over the mantel-shelf. You is jest like her as two peas in the pod and I reckin I'll have to take a stick to you like I did to yo' father when he was most growed up and stole all the fruitcake I had done baked in July fer Christmas," she said with a wide smile of great affection upon her very large mouth.

"I beg that you put under a key that cake, beloved Madam Kizzie," I made answer to her with also a laugh.

"Never was no key to nothing in this house, chile," she answered to me. "I 'lowed to the Gener'l that he had oughter git a lock and key fer this here flowered silk dress in the glass case on the wall dat de ole Mis' wore at the ball where she met up with Mas' Carruthers, but they do say that she comes back and walks as a ha'nt all dressed in it and these here slippers and stockings and folderols in the carved box on the table here under her picture. Is you 'fraid of ha'nts, honey?"

"I will not be afraid of this beautiful Grandmamma in this dress of so great magnificence, my good Kizzie," I made answer to her with more of courage than I at that moment felt.

"Well, it's only in case of a death in the house that she - Lands alive, am that my cake burning?" With which exclamation the good Kizzie left me to the company of the beautiful Grandmamma.

After having unpacked and nicely put away all of the apparel from my two large bags, the fine Bonbon retired below to answer a summons from good Kizzie, and left me alone for the first time since I had opened my eyes that morning while being whirled in the railway train down into the State of Harpeth. I looked at the hunting watch strapped to my wrist, which I had worn while traveling, and saw that it was after five o'clock, and I felt that I must sleep before dining, if for only a moment.

Thereupon I immediately climbed slowly and awk-wardly out of that gray tweed suit of clothes. I did so wonder what could be the best method of releasing one's self from trousers. It is a feat of balance to stand on one foot and remove one portion of the two sides of the trousers, and yet it is an entanglement to drop the two portions upon the floor and attempt to step out of them with the shoes upon your feet. Having succeeded in getting out of them the last night when prone upon the sleeping shelf of the railroad train, without injury to them, I again prostrated myself upon the huge bed in my room and disentangled myself from them while in that position.

After having completely disrobed I took the bath of the temperature of milk that Nannette is accustomed to administer to me, inserted myself in the very lovely 'wedding' garments for sleeping that Mr. G. Slade had so admired, and sank into deep slumber upon the large bed with a silk covering beflowered like the skirt of a lady's dress upon me.

"Well, well, you young sleepyhead, up and into your clothes, sir. We are late for the Capitol now," were the words I heard in what seemed almost the first moment after I had closed my eyes. Behold, my Uncle, the General Robert, fully dressed, stood beside the bed and a morning sun was shining through the windows. I had slept through a long night like a small child upon the bosom of the bed of my beautiful Grandmamma who smiled down upon me.

"Oh, my Uncle Robert, how much time is it that I have to make my toilet?" I begged of him as I sat up and made a rubbing of my eyes.

"Less than an hour, sir, to get out of that heathenish toggery that the men of your generation have substituted for the honest nightshirt, into proper garments, and eat your breakfast. I'll call you when I am ready to go."

It was very little more than the hour my Uncle, the General Robert, had given to me, that I consumed in the accomplishment of a very difficult toilet in a suit of very beautiful brown cheviot which the good man in New York from whom I had procured it had said to be for very especial morning wear. To my good Kizzie I gave a great uneasiness that I did not consume the very elaborate meal that resembled a dinner, which she had ready for the Bonbon to serve to me, and desired only a cup of her coffee and two very small pieces of white bread called biscuits.

"All the Carruthers men folks is friends with their food, they is," she admonished me.

"At luncheon, my Kizzie, just watch me," I said to her in nice United States words as I departed with my Uncle, the General Robert, to the Capitol of the State of Harpeth, which is a tall building set on an equally tall hill.

I found much business awaiting me in the form of making a correct translation of all of the letters in a very large portfolio, all of which were pertaining to that very tiresome animal, the mule. But I made not very much progress, for a very large number of gentlemen came into the office of my Uncle, the General Robert, and to all of them I must be presented.

In fact, in all of what remained of that entire week, for most of my moments in the Capitol I was having very painful shakes of the hand given to me and receiving assurances of my great resemblance to my honored father.

All of which I did greatly enjoy, but nothing was of so

much pleasure to me as the visits I accomplished into the office of that Gouverneur Faulkner with messages of importance from my Uncle, the General Robert.

It was with a very fine and cold smile of friendliness that he at first received me, as I stood with humble attention before his desk upon my first mission to him, but with each message I perceived that the stars in his eyes, so hid beneath his brows, shone upon me with a greater interest.

And in observing the many heavy burdens that pressed upon his strong shoulders until at the close of each day a whiteness was over his very beautiful face, I grew to desire that I could make some little things for him easier. I sought to so do and I discovered that it was possible to beguile many very heavy persons to tell to me what it was they wished to impose upon him.

I took upon a long ride in the car of my Uncle, the General Robert, that Road Commissioner, who was making a trouble for my Gouverneur Faulkner about taking much money from the sum that he desired to be voted for use on the roads of the State of Harpeth, thus making my Gouverneur Faulkner not beloved of the people in the country around the capital city, and when I returned him I had used many beguilements in the way of flattery about the superiority of the roads of America to the roads of all of the world, and had also jolted him to such an extent that he did write a nice letter to my Gouverneur Faulkner asking that that money be not voted less but even more, so as to "beat out the world with the roads of Harpeth."

"Good boy," was the reward that I got from my Gouverneur Faulkner for that feat, and a smile that was of such a loveliness that it lasted me all of the day.

Also I made a hard work for myself in saving that Gouverneur Faulkner by much flattery from a large lady who was anxious that he sign a paper by which all women might vote that no more whiskey for mint julep should exist. I very willingly put the name of Mr. Robert Carruthers to the paper, for I do not like those juleps, and I persuaded the nice large lady that she go in that car of my Uncle, the General Robert, with me away from the proximity to my chief, the Gouverneur Faulkner, to a place in the city where we could drink that ice cream soda water that I do so love.

That lady was very like many other persons who came to see my Gouverneur and whom I persuaded to make me much exhaustion instead of him. It was while telling him of the lady and the two very delicious soda ice creams that he very suddenly interrupted me with a nice smile that had in it a small warmth like the first glow of a fire, and said:

"Robert, I'm going to ask the General to lend you to me for a couple of weeks while I am so pressed. Buzz can do more for him than you do and - and, well, just looking at you and hearing you tell about the flies you brush from my wearied brow, rests me. Report to me to-morrow instead of to him. I know it will be all right, for he really needs Buzz. Now you run home and get ready for one great time at this party I'm giving to you to-night. And, Robert, remember to tell me everything the flies say, translated in your United States."

"I will and I go, my Gouverneur Faulkner," I made an answer to him with a laugh in which I did not show entirely all of the pleasure I experienced when I discovered I was to be in the place of his secretary, that fine Buzz Clendenning.

And with much haste I took my departure from the Capitol of the State of Harpeth to Twin Oaks in the car of my Uncle, the General Robert, for I knew that upon this evening I must make a new and terrible toilet and I would require much time thereto.

The good old Nannette and my Governess Madam Fournet have always taught me that the art of a lovely woman's toilet could not be performed in less than two hours, and I felt that I had better begin in the way to which I was accustomed and go as far as I could in that direction, then finish in the manly manner which would now be of a necessity to me.

The good Bonbon, whom I now know is called Sam, had laid out my evening apparel, from the queer dancing shoes with flat heels to a very stiff and high collar, upon a couch in the huge room, and after my bath I began to put them upon me with as much rapidity as was possible to me. For a few moments all went well, even up to having tucked the fine and very stiff white linen shirt garment into the silky black cloth trousers, but a trouble arose when I put upon myself the beautiful long coat that is in the shape of a raven, which the American gentleman wears for evening toilet. My shoulders were sufficiently broad to hold it nicely in place and it fell with a gracefulness upon my hips, but at my waist it collapsed on account of a slimness in that locality. The fit of the tweed, which had been like to that of a bag, had been very correct and had not revealed the curve of waist, but now it was manifest.

"What is it that you must do, Roberta, to disguise your roundness of a young woman? All is lost!" I said to myself in despair. Then a thought came to me. I had never been habited in a corset in my life on account of a prejudice entertained to that garment by my Nannette, but I bethought me to remove that shirt and also the silk one underneath and swath about me one of the heavy towels of the bath. Immediately I did so and fastened it in place with a needle and thread from the gentleman's traveling case that I found in the pocket of my bag. Over it I then drew the silk undershirt and then that of fine linen, before again putting myself into the black raven's dress. Behold, all roundness and slimness had disappeared and when the collar was added I could see that I was as beautifully habited as either Mr. Peter Scudder or that Mr. Saint Louis of the boat.

"Roberta of Grez and Bye," I said to myself as I looked into the tall mirror, "it is indeed a sorrow to you that you cannot make your courtesy to that Gouverneur Faulkner habited in the white lace and tulle garment that is in those trunks which you have lost in that New York, with your throat that your Russian Cossack has said was like a lily at the blush of dawn, bare to his eyes, but you are a nice, clean, upstanding American boy who can be his friend. You must be and you must play the game."

And in the language of that Mr. Willie Saint Louis, it was "some game."

CHAPTER IX

"O'ER THE LAND OF THE FREE "

I have a desire to know if it is into the life of every person there comes one night which he is never to forget until death and perhaps even after. I do not know; but I am sure that I shall always keep the memory of the night upon which Mr. Robert Carruthers of Grez and Bye was introduced to the friends of his ancestors. It is my jewel that seems a drop of heart's blood that I will wear forever hid in my breast.

At dinner I sat beside the Gouverneur Williamson Faulkner and tears came into my eyes as he rose from beside me at the head of the table and said:

"Ladies and gentlemen, I ask you to drink to the homecoming of Robert Carruthers, my friend, your friend, and everybody his friends."

And from that long table there came to me such beautiful and loving smiles over the glasses of champagne that they went to my head instead of the wine I could not even sip because of the tears in my throat. It was as that day upon the great ship when I saw fulfilled before my eyes my vow to my Capitaine, the Count de Lasselles: "Friends for France." I sat still for a long minute; then I rose to my feet with my glass in my hand.

"I cannot make to you a speech, but I beg that I may say to you words that were of the first taught to my infant tongue and which I last repeated in an old convent close to the trenches in France."

Then in the rich voice which has come to me from the deep singing of my mother I repeated very quietly:

"Oh - say, can you see, by the dawn's early light, What so proudly we hailed at the twilight's last gleaming; Whose broad stripes and bright stars, thro' the perilous fight, O'er the ramparts we watched, were so gallantly streaming? And the rocket's red glare, the bombs bursting in air, Gave proof thro' the night that our flag was still there -"

through to the last words which had fallen from my lips as I had taken my father's dying kiss:

"O'er the land of the free and the home of the brave."

Though I had not told them of it, I do believe there was not a heart among those kind people which did not know of that last moment in the old convent and I could see it in tears dashed aside as they all rose and sang the last strain of the American song, with the musicians in the anteroom leading them.

And as they sang that most wonderful song, Gouverneur Faulkner laid his arm across my shoulder, and the comfort of its strength gave to me the courage to send back all the smiles that were sent to me, as that funny Mr. Buzz Clendenning said while they

Maria Thompson Daviess

seated themselves:

"Gee, but L'Aiglon is the real un-hyphenated brand of old Uncle Sam, Jr."

"Thank God that firebrand isn't a girl," I heard my Uncle, the General Robert, say to most lovely Mademoiselle Susan, in a corn-colored gown of fine line, who sat at his side.

"I'm so grateful to you, General, that he is a boy," I heard her say in the deepest respect and regard for my Uncle, the General Robert.

"I don't doubt at all, Madam, that you will succeed in making me wish that he had been born a girl or not at all," was the kind reply that he made to her nicely spoken gratitude as we laughed into each other's eyes across the table.

"I hope so," was the answer with which Mademoiselle Sue comforted him.

"And now what have you to say to me, boy, the oldest friend you've got in America, who hasn't seen you for days - that have been too long," said that Madam Whitworth, who was seated at my side, and as she spoke she turned one lovely bare shoulder in the direction of my Uncle, the General Robert, and the beautiful Mademoiselle Sue and also Buzz, as if to shut them away from her and me in a little space of world just for two people.

"I can say with truth, Madam, that your loveliness to-night is but the flowering of my suspicions of it that morning upon the railroad train," I answered her in words that were a very nice translation of what that fine young Cossack had once said to me at the Chateau de Grez of my own flowering into rose chiffon after an afternoon's hunting with him in corduroys. And in truth I spoke no falsehood to that Madam Whitworth, for she was of a very great beauty of body, very much of which was in view from a scantiness of bodice that I had never seen excelled in any ballroom in France.

"I knew you for a poet from that adorable black mop which I see you have very nicely plastered in an exact imitation of Buzz Clendenning's red one," she answered me with a laugh. "Follow me from the ballroom just after supper at midnight for a half hour's chat alone in a place I know; and don't let either the General or the Governor see you," she then said in an undertone as the Gouverneur Faulkner bent forward and began a laughing conversation with her.

"I will," I answered her under my breath, and I leaned back in my chair so that the Gouverneur Faulkner could more conveniently converse with her. And to that end he placed his arm across the back of my chair, and thus I sat in his embrace with my shoulder pressed into his.

I do not know exactly what it was that happened in the depths of me, but suddenly the daredevil rose from those depths and knew herself for a very strong woman filled to the brim with a primitive, savage cunning with which to fight the beautiful woman at my side for the honor of the man whose strong heart I could feel beating against my woman's breast strapped down under its garment of man's attire. And that cunning showed me that I would have a hundredfold better opportunity to do her and her schemes against him and against France to the death in my garments and character of a man, than I could have had if I had come into his and her world as the beautiful young Roberta, Marquise of Grez and Bye. Then for those hated garments of a raven my heart beat so high with gratitude that I moved again forward from the arm of His Excellency for fear that he might feel the tumult even through that strong towel of the bath which I had sewed above it, and be in wonderment as to its cause.

"Here's to your first duel with a woman in which you use a man's weapons, Roberta, Marquise of Grez and Bye, and see that you score - for him - and for France!" I said to myself as we rose from the table and with the other men I bowed the ladies from the room.

"At midnight," I whispered while I bent for a second to kiss the hand of the beautiful Madam Whitworth as she left the room. As I raised my head from the salutation I encountered the eyes of the Gouverneur Faulkner, which looked into mine with an expression of calm question. And for a moment I let the woman rise superior to the raven attire and I looked back into those eyes, in which I saw the mystery of the dawn star, as would have gazed Roberta, Marquise of Grez and Bye, had she been attired in the white tulle and lace abandoned in that New York; then I beat her back down into my heart and gave him the smile of fealty that was his due from Robert Carruthers, his friend, along with one similar, to the fine young Buzz Clendenning, who at that moment came to my side and claimed my attention.

"You score with Sue. I'm to be the gracious little home city host and give up any dances your Marquisity may choose with her. Sue foxes like she was born in a fox hole under a hollow log, but she tangoes like the original Emperor Tang himself, so go ahead and suit yourself. Don't mind me. I'm the loving little playmate."

"That Mademoiselle Sue is so much of a peach that I am inclined to request the receptacle of cream that I may devour her," I then made answer to him in as many of the words of enthusiasm over a nice lady as I could remember that Mr. George Slade of Detroit to have used over the "skirt" in Louisville in the Country of Kentucky.

"Good, Bobby! I'll have to go tell Sue that before she is two minutes older. I wouldn't want her to live five minutes longer without having heard it. Sue's dead sure to tell the rest of the girl bunch, so I hope you have a supply where that came from, for they'll all cry for 'em. There's the Governor making towards the door and Mrs. Pat, who is always waiting at the gate for him, so come, let me lead you to the dance." With which my nice Buzz and I followed the Gouverneur Faulkner and the other gentlemen across the hall into the long salon of the Mansion, whose floors were polished like unto a lake of ice, for dancing.

In Touraine it is said that a nice lady fairy comes for a visit of inspection at the *berceau* - in America it is cradle - of each small human that is born, and gives to it a beautiful gift if propitiations are made for it to please her. To that end sweetmeats and nice presents are placed beside the small infant with which to beguile the good opinion of that fairy. I would I could be that exalted person and able to visit every small infant born a female in all of the world. And the gift I would give to her, there in her sleep, would be to one time in her life attend a ball in the raven attire of a man in the city of Hayesville of America. I could bestow no greater gift.

The hours that followed my entry into the ballroom in the Mansion of the exalted Gouverneur Faulkner were like minutes of time that dropped from a golden clock of joy. I danced on feet that were strong wings to glide over a floor that was a many colored cloud from the reflection of the soft lights and the silken skirts which ruffled over it. And, what was most enjoyable to me in this case, I glided in whatever direction pleased me and took with me the armful of cloud, which was the girl with whom I was dancing, on long swoops of my own will, instead of being led in my flights by another as had always before been the case with my dancing. It was the most of a joy that I had ever experienced. And as I so enjoyed that freedom I did not know how it was that I should have such a feeling of dissatisfaction when I beheld that beautiful Madam Whitworth dancing within the arms of the Gouverneur Williamson Faulkner. I blushed that I should be so unworthy, with such an unreasonable fury in my heart, and I looked away so that I seemed not to see the smile that he sent to me over the head of the very sweet Belle girl in blue ruffles and silver slippers I was guiding past him in the trot of a fox.

"Yes, Sue Tomlinson *is* as lovely as a ripe peach, isn't she?" asked Mademoiselle Blue Cloud of me as I lowered her almost to the floor over my arm, slid her four steps to the left then trotted her two back and two forward; and her tone had a very sweet demand of wistfulness in it as she looked up into my eyes and pressed very close to that protecting towel of the bath.

For an instant I could not think of one single bonbon of compliment to offer the lady and I wished I had sat up all of the night to talk to that Mr. G. Slade of Detroit in the railroad train and had had my nice gray lady friend in the Ritz-Carlton there with her notebook to transcribe the many pleasing things he reported himself to have said to the ladies whom he called "skirts." Then nice Lord Chisholm came all the way from England into my memory to assist me in my difficulty. I translated from him freely in this manner:

"Aw, on me word, you *are* a ripping good sort and I could take you on for the whole evening if you'd let me. What?"

"I wish I could," she answered and by that time I had thought out a nice little squeeze for her very pretty waist in its silver girdle under my arm. Then I had to put her into the arms of a nice young man named Miles Menefee. To get my breath and to think up some more of the compliments that had been given to me for my pleasure in the past, I made my retreat behind a very large palm that was in the corner of the room, and out upon a wide balcony which hung over a moonlit garden across which I could see dim hills in the moonlight.

"Girls of all nations are granddaughters of the same Monsieur Satan, I suspect," I made remark to myself as I inhaled the perfume of the flower garments of the spring garden below. "I must take a great care that I do not -"

"And then, boy, you'll slip on the thin ice when you least expect it," came in the deep voice of the Gouverneur Faulkner from a shadow at my elbow. "I sometimes think that they love us just to double-cross our life's ambitions, but don't you begin to suspect that for years to come."

"A man's life must be rooted in the heart of a woman if it would bear fruit, Monsieur le Gouverneur," I found myself saying as in the person of the Roberta, Marquise of Grez and Bye, I drew myself to my full height with pride in defense of my own sex. "A man doubts that to his own dishonor."

"Yes, but it must be a pure heart that nourishes a man to his full fruitage - and, boy, don't you take even a sip - until you are sure there are such founts of refreshment."

"I would that you could look into my heart, my Gouverneur Faulkner," I said as I raised my hand and laid it against the raven garment that covered my soft breast that was rent with pain at the sadness of his voice and his deep eyes. "There you would see the heart of one -" Suddenly I stopped in the deepest dismay and the daredevil quaked in her trousers.

"I would probably see the heart of - shall I say, Galahad Junior? God bless you, boy, you are refreshing." And he laughed as he laid his strong hands on my shoulder and gave to me a good shake.

"Are you my comrade Launcelot?" I asked him with a sudden fierce pain again in my breast under the raven coat at the thought of what that Queen of the yellow hair had done to that brave Knight of the Round Table of King Arthur.

"I don't think I'll answer your - your impertinence, boy.

Just keep foxing with Sue and Belle and the rest of the posy girls and - and keep away from the pools - of - of other eyes." And after another shaking he turned me towards the door of that ballroom of lights and music.

At the command of the Gouverneur Faulkner there was nothing I could do but go back to the ballroom and to float for more minutes in the land of cloud with the "girl bunch," as my friend that Buzz has named them; but at supper I took my seat at the table with that beautiful Madam Whitworth and her husband of the very drooping black mustache and eyes that looked at all places except into those of the person addressing him. And at that moment I made this resolve to myself: "That Gouverneur Launcelot may ride far out of the white road, but I intend to run at his stirrup." And I found that it required swift running, for the road led - shall I say - into "tall timbers."

It is with a burning of countenance that arises from a hot shame, which I do not even to this moment exactly understand, that I recall to my mind that half hour which Mr. Robert Carruthers of Grez and Bye spent with the beautiful Madam Patricia Whitworth in one of the deep windows that looked from the private study of His Excellency of the State of Harpeth, over into the great hills that surround the city. Things happened in this wise: That Madam Whitworth made the commencement of our duel of intelligences by assuming that I was a simple French infant before whom she could dangle the very sweet bonbon of affection and take away from it a treasure that it held in the hollow of its hand as a sacred trust. That Madam Whitworth did not realize that instead of a very small young boy from gay Paris, whose eyes were closed like those of a very young cat, she was dealing with the very wicked girl

Maria Thompson Daviess

who placed the word "devil" behind the word "dare," speaking in the language of that Mr. Willie Saint Louis when he informed me that he was the man who had so placed the "go" behind Chicago while on a visit to that city. I was that girl.

CHAPTER X

VITRIOL AND THE HOODOO

"I suppose it is absurd for a staid old matron like myself to be jealous, really jealous, at seeing a child like you being consumed alive by a lot of simpering misses in pink and blue chiffon pinafores, who ought to be in their nursery cots asleep, but I have been and am, boy. Did you forget that I was your oldest friend while Sue Tomlinson fed you sweets out of her hand?" And as she spoke she seated herself in the exact center of the window seat and motioned me to place myself in the portion of the left side that remained. I inserted myself into the space that was so indicated and laid my arm along the window ledge behind her very much undressed back, so that I might give to my lungs space to expand for air. I think that arrangement made very much for the comfort of the beautiful Madam Patricia, for she immediately appropriated that arm as a cushion for her undraped shoulders. We being thus comfortably wedged, the warfare began.

"All week I've been thinking about you, you wonderful boy, and wondering just what you have been doing and what has been doing to you. The General is so - so incomprehensible in his attitude towards you and yours. All these years he has been" - and as she spoke she looked up into my eyes and pressed slightly

Maria Thompson Daviess

towards me - "uncompromising, hasn't he?"

"Yes, Madam, I do find my Uncle, the General Robert, to be, as you say, uncompromising," I answered as I looked down at her with a smile. "But you are not like that, are you, beautiful Madam Whitworth? You will compromise yourself, will you not?"

"Don't use English words so carelessly, my dear, until you are less ignorant of their meaning," she reproved me as she sat erect and gave to my lungs an inch more breathing space. I had heard that large lady of the State of Cincinnati on the ship say that a nice lady from a place called Kansas, and whom everyone gave the title of Mrs. Grass because of a disagreeable husband who was not dead, "compromised" herself with a very much drinking gentleman from Boston because she sat in a small space with him behind the chimney for smoke from the engine, and I thought it was a nice word to fit into the conversation with Madam Whitworth at that time. And I think it did fit better than I had quite intended that it should. I saw offense and I hastened to make a peace so that I should learn all that I wanted to know from her while letting her learn all that I did not know from me.

"I beg that you pardon me, beautiful Madam, and teach me the English words to say that will express all of - of the most wonderful things that I think of you. What is the one word that expresses the beauty of the blue flowers in crystal that I said your eyes to be, to myself, the first time I looked into them upon that railroad train when you rescued me from the black taffeta lady?" And as I was at that moment speaking the exact truth I spoke with a great ardor.

"I rather think that offsets Sue Tomlinson's 'cream jug' compliment - and you *are* a dear," she answered as she again diminished the space for my lung action. "I hear the dear General has turned you over to the Governor completely. What do you think of him?" she asked as if to manufacture conversation.

"Yes, I was made a gift to him last week, and I do not think very much of that Gouverneur," I made answer with excellent falseness, because I had had no thoughts since my presentation to that Gouverneur Faulkner that were not of him. I had obtained the uncomplimentary remark upon the ship, from the lady of Cincinnati, who said it about the doctor of the seasickness from which she suffered.

"Between you and me, boy - if anything, even an opinion, can be wedged between us - I think the Governor is a great, overrated stupid, encouraged in his denseness by the dear General whose ideas have - have - er - rather solidified with age. I rather pity you for having to have all of your opinions and policies of life moulded by them. Yes, it is a pity." And she sighed very near to my cheek.

"Will you not mould me to some extent yourself, beautiful flower-eyed Madam?" I asked of her with great gentleness, and did administer a nice little pressure to her shoulders like I had adventured upon the waist of the beautiful Belle in blue and silver dress which Madam Whitworth had named a pinafore.

"You are a perfect dear, and I will help you all I can. Just come and tell me all of your difficulties and I'll try and smooth them away for you. I suppose you will find it easy to translate their French documents for them about this very boring mule deal. I have had to do it and I am glad to turn the burden of it all over to you. You may have some trouble with the English technicalities and perhaps you had best bring them in to me and I'll run over them to see that you get them straight. Only don't let the General know that I am helping you, for I verily believe the old dear thinks I am a nihilist ready to blow the Governor or any of his other old mules into a thousand bits."

"I thank you, beautiful Madam Whitworth, for your offer of assistance, and I will avail myself of it at the first opportunity. Is it at your house that we can be alone?" I questioned with a daring smile that would serve both for a purpose of coquetry and also to ascertain if I would encounter in a call upon her that very disagreeable appearing gentleman, Mr. Jefferson Whitworth, who is the husband to his very beautiful wife.

"Come any afternoon at four o'clock and telephone me before you come so that I can get rid of anybody who happens to be around. And be sure to bring any work you have for me to help you with. That's the only way I can excuse an ancient matron like myself for keeping you even for a few minutes away from the pinafores." And she looked into my eyes with a sigh for her antiquity. In the language of that Mr. Willie Saint Louis I knew it was "up to me," and I "handed the dame one."

"In my country, beautiful Madam, the fruit is much more regarded than the bud," is what I presented to her.

" You are delicious, " she laughed as she again

diminished my breathing space. "I cannot see why the dear General has been so violent in his prejudice against all things from France. You must try to win him over, especially as he is letting his prejudice to France, if you can call downright hatred that, stand in the way of lending his aid in doing a great service to your poor, struggling, brave army, while at the same time reaping a profit to his own State. Has he told you anything of this mule deal he is forcing Governor Faulkner to hold up on some others who want to do a service to France?" As she questioned me, the beautiful Madam's eyes became much narrower and I could observe that she watched me with intentness for any sign of intelligence. I gave her none.

"Will you not tell me, my Madam of the blue flower eyes, about all of the matter? It will be of great benefit to me to understand it all from you, for my Uncle the General Robert is a man of few words and I am not a man of much business intelligence." And as I spoke I regarded her with a great and beseeching humility.

And there, in the Mansion of the Gouverneur of the State of Harpeth himself, that lovely woman did unfold to me the most wonderful plan for the most enormous robbery of both her own government and mine - or should I say of both of my governments? - that it could be in the power of mortal mind to conceive. It was a beautiful, reasonable, generous, patriotic, sympathetic drama of the gigantic war mule and it had only one tiny, hidden obscure line in one of its verses, but in that line lay all of dishonor that could come to a man and a State who should allow a smaller nation fighting for its life and its honor to be defrauded of one of the supplies which were of a deadly necessity for its success. I think I even saw the dastardly scheme more plainly than did my Uncle, the General Robert, for I had listened with more than one ear while my Capitaine, the Count de Lasselles, explained to wee Pierre some of the details of supplying the army of the Republique. I think he had talked of things that the little one could not understand just to make an ease of the pressure of all of his business upon his troubled mind and breaking heart. And as Madam Whitworth talked I could hear my Pierre's brave voice as he always gave assurances to his sad idol.

"All of plenty is in America, and she will give to France."

And here sat great strong Roberta, the Marquise of Grez and Bye, holding in the hollow of her arm a beautiful American woman who had herself contrived a monstrous plan to let a quantity of the lifeblood of France to turn into gold for her own vain uses. If to throttle her then and there with my bare strong hands had insured the great big needful mules to France, and saved the honor of my Gouverneur of the State of Harpeth, and my Uncle, the General Robert, I think I might have had a great temptation to administer that death to her; but instead I held her now closer in my arm and I began to plot her to death in any other way I could discover, so that her intrigue should die with her.

"Of a truth, beautiful Madam, the poor old Uncle, the General Robert, must not be allowed to interfere with such a beautiful plan as you have for supplying those very fine strong mules from the State of Harpeth to poor struggling France, and I will join with you in convincing the stupid Gouverneur Faulkner that such must not be the case. You will direct me, will you not? I am very young and I have but so lately come to this land that I do not know - I do not feel exactly what you call at home." And I spoke again with beseeching humility.

"We'll do it for France together, boy," she whispered as she turned in my arm and pressed herself against my raven attire above my heart held in restraint by that towel of the bath. "And then you can claim from me any - reward - you - "

Just at this lovely moment, when the beautiful Madam Whitworth had thrown herself into my arms and I had been obliged by my cunning to hold her there instead of flinging her to the floor as I naturally desired, there arrived at the door of the room which we were occupying with our plotting, my tall and awful Uncle, the General Robert, and looked down upon us with the lightnings of a storm in his eyes. Then, before I could make exclamation and betray his presence to the lady in my arms, whose back was turned in his direction, he had disappeared. Did I betray that presence to the lady? I did not. I decided that it would be much to the advantage of the affair to have the lady in ignorance of his knowledge.

"You must go now, boy," she said at about the moment in which I could no longer keep my dissembling alive. "Send the Governor in here to me, for it is about the time I had promised to dance with him. I want to talk with him and try to make him see some at least of this matter in the right light. Go; and come to me to-morrow at four - for - for France."

I went and it was with much joy in the going. I stopped at a tall window to get into my lungs a very deep supply of atmosphere and also to take counsel with myself.

"Mr. Robert Carruthers," I said to myself, "you are in what that Mr. G. Slade of Detroit said to be a 'hell of a fix' when the nice aunt of that beautiful and refined 'skirt' of Saint Joseph, Missouri, discovered her to be in his embrace of farewell. I cannot tell to my Uncle, the General Robert, that it is that I, a woman of honor, have planned for myself, a man of dishonor, to betray a woman into his hands, and I shall receive from him what that Buzz Clendenning calls to be a 'dressing down.' But I must go to send to Madam Delilah now the great Gouverneur of the State of Harpeth and for what she does to him that is unholy she will answer to Robert Carruthers or - or Roberta, Marquise of Grez and Bye." And then immediately I went to deliver the summons of Madam Whitworth to the Gouverneur Faulkner and I did not look into his face as I spoke the words, but waited with my eyes cast down to the floor until he dismissed me.

Then after that very painful hour of intrigue I allowed to Mr. Robert Carruthers another of very delightful gayety with all of the "chiffon pinafore" ladies upon the ballroom floor. I have in my blood that gayety which led some of my ancestors to laugh and compliment each other and play piquet up even to the edge of the guillotine, and I refused to see the countenance of my Uncle, the General Robert, regarding me from the door in the end of the ballroom. I considered that an hour of pleasure was a sacred thing not to be interfered with, and I danced with that sweet Sue Tomlinson right past the edge of his toes while I could feel the delicious giggle within her, which was answering that within me, at his fierce regard of us both.

"He'll eat you up before daylight, Mr. Carruthers," she said as she cast a sweet and loving glance at my Uncle, the General Robert, which, I could see as I lowered her over my arm and slid away from him, was giving to him much nice fury.

"I will request that Madam black Kizzie to make a good cream gravy to me," I made answer to her with merriment. "I am very tender," I added with audacity that I was learning with such a rapidity that I trembled for the reputation of Mr. Robert Carruthers, and as I spoke the words I gave to her a little embrace in a turn of the dance. It should not have been done, but if that sweet Sue had known that a very lonely girl danced in that raven garb of a man, who wanted to hold her close for her comforting, she would have forgiven it, I feel sure. That Sue is a young woman of such a good sense that I must forever cherish her.

"Don't do that again, Bobby Carruthers," she said, looking up at me with a lovely seriousness in her honest young eyes. "I know you are French, and queer, but - but don't -" After a little she added: "We are going to be grand friends, aren't we?" "Yes, lovely Sue, and I beg of you pardon," I answered her with all of the friendliness of Roberta, Marquise of Grez and Bye, in my eyes and voice, which seemed to give to her a beautiful satisfaction.

"Good! I'll tell you what let's do. You come by for me to-morrow afternoon and I'll go with you to the Capitol and I'll beard the General Lion in his den and ask him to let us be friends, and then we'll take him out to the Confederate Soldiers' Home for 'flags down' - it mellowed him so once, when I was about ten, that he let me trot home beside him holding his hand, though he didn't speak to me for a week after. Want to?" I did enjoy the mischief in those merry eyes that I laughed into.

"I'll steal his big car and come and help you - what do you say? - kidnap my Uncle, the General Robert," I answered her with delight as I released her into the arms of that Buzz Clendenning before the fox had been more than half trotted.

"Go pick roses out of your own garden, L'Aiglon," he said as he slid her away from me.

And for the reason that I was very slightly fatigued and also slightly warm from being obliged to dance in the very heavy swathings of a gentleman, when I had been accustomed to the coolness of chiffon and tulle and thin lace of a lady, I went again into the broad hall and to the wide window that looked away to those comforting blue hills. Below me the garden was coming out of a veil of mist as the moon, which was now very old, came slowly up from behind the dim ridge of hills that my Uncle the General Robert had told me to be called Paradise Ridge. All the spring flowers below me seemed to be sending up to me greetings of perfumes and the tall purple and white lilac flowers waved plumes of friendliness at me, while large round pink blossoms that I think are called peonies, nodded and beckoned to me with sweet countenances. I felt that they were flower friends who in their turn were saying messages of welcome to the lonely girl who had come across the dark waters to them and in my throat I began to hum that "Say can you see -" Star Spangled hymn to them, and was just preparing to step from the window onto a balcony and descend to them, when a movement of human beings caught my eye upon the side of that balcony and I paused in the darkness of the window curtain. What did I see?

A man stood at the rail of the balcony in the dim moonlight and he was speaking to a woman whom his broad shoulders hid from me. The man was the Gouverneur Faulkner of the State of Harpeth and in a moment I discovered the identity of the lady with him.

"And now, can't you see, you great big stupid man, what an opportunity I have procured for all of you?" was the question that came in the soft voice of the beautiful Madam Patricia Whitworth. "All my life I have worked just to get a little ease and comfort, carrying the burden of Jeff in his incompetency strapped to my shoulders, and now you, who know how I've suffered and slaved, are going to take it all from me when it is just within my reach, and all from no earthly reason than a fancied scruple of honor which that old doddering woman-hater imposes on you. I cannot believe that you would so treat me." And there were sobs in her words that were wooing and compelling.

"I cannot do a thing that my Secretary of State and his lawyers declare unconstitutional, Patricia," answered the voice of the Gouverneur Faulkner, in which were notes of pain. "You know how it pains me - my God, don't tempt me to - " His voice shook as I saw the beautiful, bare white arms of Madam Whitworth raise themselves and go about his neck like great white grappling hooks from which he was unable to defend himself.

"Am I to have nothing from life - no ease or luxury and

no - love or -" Her voice ended in sobs as she pressed her head down into his shoulder as his arm folded about her to prevent that she should fall.

"Patricia -" the deep voice of the strong man was beginning to say as I was starting to spring forward in his defense and to do - I do not know what - when a firm grasp was laid upon my shoulder and I was turned away from the window into the light of the wide hall and found my Uncle, the General Robert, looking down into my flashing eyes with a great and very cool calmness.

"Young man," he said as he gave to me a very powerful shake, "all women are poison but some are vitriol and others just - Oh, well, paregoric. Go out there and take another dose of that soothing syrup labeled Susan Tomlinson, before I take you home, and you - keep - away - from - vitriol - or - I'll - break - your - hot - young - head. Vitriol, mind you!" With which command my Uncle, the General Robert, strode down the hall in the direction of the smoking room and left me blinking in the lights of the wide hall.

"Little Mas' Robert," came in a soft voice at my elbow as I stood tottering, "is you got a picture of yo' mudder you could show Cato some day when the General ain't lookin'. 'Fore I dies I wants to set my eyes on de woman dat drawed little Mas' Henry away from us all. Dey *is* such a thing in dis hard old world as love what you goes 'crost many waters' to git, and he shorely got it." And I looked into the eyes of that old black man to find a truth that all the white humans about me, myself included, were acting in the terms of a lie.

Before I could answer the old man, in through the

window came the Gouverneur Faulkner and the beautiful Madam Whitworth, and from his white face set in sternness and hers with its smile of the opening rose upon its red mouth I could not tell whether his honor had been slain or had been spared for another round.

"I'll want you in my office at the Capitol at eleven tomorrow, Robert," he said to me, and there was a cold sternness in his glance as they passed by me and the old Cato into the ballroom.

"At four," murmured the beautiful Madam Whitworth as she swept past me with a soft smile but in a tone of voice too low for any ears save my own and I think of the old Cato's.

For a very short moment the old black man detained me as he searched one of the pockets of his long gray coat and then he handed to me a tiny flat parcel apparently folded in some kind of thin red cloth.

"Wear that in your left shoe, honey, day and night. You'll need it if she's got her eye on you," he said as he hurried away from me into the smoking room.

After disrobing that night, or rather in the early morning of the following day, I investigated the contents of that package. In it were a gray feather off of an apparently very nice chicken, a very old and rusty pin bent in two places and a flat little black seed I had never before beheld.

I gazed at the package for several long moments, then I put back upon my left foot the silk sock I had removed, placed the token of old Cato within it under my heel, dived into that large bed of my ancestors and in the darkness covered up my head tightly with the silk comforter.

CHAPTER XI

BUSINESS AND PIE

That Mr. Buzz Clendenning has in the composition of his nature a very large portion of nice foolishness which makes the heart of a lonely person most comfortable. He decided, upon that very first day of our introduction, that I was to be as a small brother to him who was much loved but also to be much joked about a quaintness which he chose to call "French greenness," and for which I was most grateful because with that excuse I could cover all mistakes that arose from my being a girl who was ignorant of the exact methods of being a man. And, also, that nice attitude towards me was of quite a contagion, for all of the young ladies and gentlemen of the city of Hayesville became the same to me and all of the time my heart was warm and rejoiced at their affection shown in banter and jokes.

The morning after that very much enjoyed dinner dance, with which the Governor Faulkner complimented my Uncle, the General Robert, through me, I was standing in front of the mirror in my room without my coat or my collar, endeavoring to reduce the wave in my black hair to the sleekness of that of my beloved Buzz, which had a difficulty because of one lock over my temple whose waywardness I had for the last few

Maria Thompson Daviess

years trained to fall upon my cheek for purposes of coquetry and which would persist in trying still to fulfill that unworthy function. And right in the center of my punishment of that lovelock with the stiff brush without a handle, which was twins with another that had come with the gentleman's traveling bag which I had purchased in New York of the nice fat gentleman in the store of clothing for men, into my room came that Buzz without any ceremony save a rap upon my door which did not allow sufficient time for any response from me. I blushed with alarm at the thought that his entrance might have come at a much earlier stage of my toilet and I made a resolve to lock the door tight in future, at the same time turning to greet him with a fine and great composure.

"Say, Bobby, are you in for side-stepping the chiefs at eleven-thirty and going with me to take a nice bunch of calicoes out to the Country Club for a little midday sandwich dance? You can eat a thin ham and fox trot at the same time. Sue and Belle and Kate Keith all want to get on to that long slide you've brought over direct from Paree. It stuck in their systems last evening and they want more. Want to go?"

"With a greatness of pleasure, but His Excellency has commanded me at eleven o'clock and will I be through the tasks at the hour for escorting those calicoes out to your Club for a dance?" I asked with great delight as I continued my operations with the brush upon the rebellious lock.

"You'll have time if you stop that primping and hustle into your collar and coat. Here, let me show you how to doctor that place where the cow licked you. Why don't you take both brushes to it? Like this!" With which Mr. Buzz took from my hand the one brush and from the high dressing table the other, for which my ignorance had discovered no use, and did then commence a vigorous assault on my enemy the curl.

"What was it you said of a cow, my Buzz?" I questioned him as I made a squirming under the vigor of his attack upon my hair.

"When hair acts up like this we call it a cowlick in United States language. See here, L'Aiglon, old boy, this hair looks as if it had at one time been curled. Did you wear it that way in Paris?" And as he asked the question he gave that side of my hair one more vigorous sweep and stood off to admire his work.

"No, my Buzz, I assure you that it was the cruelty of that cow you mention, while I was at a very tender age," I answered with a laugh into his eyes that covered nicely the blush that rose to my cheek at his accusation concerning the lovelock.

"Well, knot that tie now in a jiffy and climb into your coat. Let's get to the Capitol and give the old boys as little of our attention as they'll stand for, and then beat it for the girls. Bet my chief growls blue blazes at me over the way Sue ragged him about you last night. He'll issue a command at the point of the bayonet to me to keep you away from the bunch, and I'll agree just so as to make the slide from under easy. Come on." And while he spoke to me, that Buzz raced me down the hall of my ancestors and out into his very slim, fast car before I could get breath for speaking.

"But suppose His Excellency the Gouverneur Faulkner requires my presence beyond that half hour after eleven o'clock, my Buzz, is it that you will await me for a few short minutes?" I asked of him as we ascended the steps of the Capitol of the State of Harpeth.

"Oh, Bill won't keep you any longer than that. He'll have twenty other interviews on the string for to-day. Fifteen minutes will be about right for you; you wait for me in the General's anteroom. I'll have to get heroics before instructions. I always do. Now beat it." With which words my Buzz left me in the wide hall of the great Capitol before a door marked: "Office of the Governor."

Upon that door I knocked and it was immediately opened to me by fine black Cato, whose eyes shone in recognition of me.

"Got it in yo' shoe?" he demanded in a whisper.

"Yes, my good Cato," I responded also in a low tone of voice.

"Den pass on in to de Governor; he am waitin' fer you. You's safe, chile." And he escorted me past several gentlemen seated and standing in groups, to another door, which he opened for me and through which he motioned me to pass.

"Mr. Robert Carruthers," he announced me with the greatest ceremony. "Go in, honey," he said softly and I passed into the room whose door he closed quietly behind me.

"Good morning, Robert," said the Gouverneur Faulkner to me as I came and stood opposite him at the edge of his wide desk. And he smiled at me with a great gentleness that had also humor playing into it from the corners of his eyes and mouth. "I'm afraid that you've landed in the midst of a genuine case of American hustle this 'morning after.' Here are two lists of specifications, one in English weights and measurements and the other in French. I want you to compare them carefully, checking them as you go and then re-checking them. I want to be sure they are the same. Also make a good literal translation of any notes that may be in French and compare them with the notes in English. Do you think it can be done for me by three o'clock, in time for a conference I have at that hour?" With which request he, the Gouverneur Faulkner, handed me two large sheets of paper down which were many long columns of figures.

"*Mon Dieu*," I said to myself under my breath, for always I have had to count out the pieces of money necessary to give to Nannette for the washer of the linen at the Chateau de Grez, upon the fingers of my hands, which often seemed too few to furnish me sufficient aid. But in a small instant I had recovered my courage, which brought with it a determination to do that task if it meant my death.

"Yes, Your Excellency," I answered him with a great composure in the face of the tragedy.

"You'll find the small office between my office and that of General Carruthers empty. A ring of the bell under the desk means for you to come to me. I'll try not to interrupt you. Two rings means to go to the General. That is about all." With a wave of his hand the Gouverneur Faulkner dismissed me to my death.

With my head up in the air I turned from him and prepared to retire to my prison from which I could see no release, when again I heard his summons. He had risen and was standing beside his desk and as I turned he held out his hand into which I laid mine as he drew me near to him.

"Youngster," he said and the smile which all persons call cold was all of gentleness into my eyes, "these are going to be some hard days for us all, these next ten, and if I drive you too hard, balk, will you?"

"To the death for you I'll go, my Gouverneur Faulkner," I answered him, looking straight into his tired eyes that were so deep under the black, silver-tipped wings of his brows. I did not mean that death I had threatened myself from the mathematics in the paper, but in my heart there was something that rose and answered the sadness in his eyes with again all that savageness of a barbarian.

"Then I'll take you to the point of demise - almost - if I need you," he answered me with a laugh that hid a quiver of emotion in his voice as something that was like unto a spark shot from the depths of his eyes into the depths of mine. "Go get the papers verified and let me know when you have finished." And this time I was in reality dismissed. I went; but in my heart was a strange smoulder that the spark had kindled.

In the small room that opened off of that of the Gouverneur Faulkner, with a door that I knew to lead into the room of my Uncle, the General Robert, I seated myself at a table by a window which looked down upon the city spread at the foot of the Capitol hill lying shimmering in the young spring mists that drifted across its housetops. I laid down the papers, took a pencil from a tray close beside my hand and then faced the most dreadful of any situation that I had ever brought down upon my own head. I also faced at the same time the smiling countenance of my Buzz, who looked into the door from the room of my Uncle, the General Robert, slipped through that door and closed it gently behind him.

"Safe on first base! The old boy of the bayonets has been called to the Governor and he'll not be back before they both have luncheon sent in to them. I have taken his letters and now I'm off. What did Bill hand you?"

"Death and also destruction," I answered in an expletive often used by my father in times of a catastrophe, and with those words I showed to my Buzz the two long papers.

"Shoo, that's no big job. I looked over and verified this one myself yesterday in ten minutes. Hello, this other one is in French. Just run it through and if it is to tally, call it; and I'll hold this one. We can do it in fifteen minutes. Go ahead from the top line across." And my Buzz held the paper in his hand as he seated himself in readiness upon the corner of my desk beside me.

"Oh, my Buzz, I have such a mortification that I cannot add one to another of these long figures. When I place one number to another I must use my fingers, and in this case you see that it is impossible." Tears I did not allow in my eyes, but they were in my voice, and I looked into the eyes of my Buzz with a great terror. "What is it that I shall do? I am in disgrace."

"You complete edition of a kid, you, don't you know I can do it for you? That is, if you know what all these kilo things stand for in English. Do you?" As he spoke, that kind Buzz put his hand on my shoulder with a nice rough shake.

"I do know from my governess, Madam Fournet, and I will write it all down for you, my Buzz, for whom I feel so much gratitude for help," I answered with quickness.

"Stow the gratitude and write 'em all out. It will take us about an hour but it is good to keep calicoes waiting occasionally," he said, and did thereupon seat himself beside the table and draw to himself the two sheets of paper, while I quickly wrote out the table of French weights and measurements translated into English.

I did very much enjoy that hour in which my Buzz labored with a pencil and a great industry while I called to him the list of long figures and then verified as he showed me the units upon the page in the French language. He made jokes at me between workings while he attended his cigarette and we, together, had much laughter.

"There are just three places where these figures disagree and I have marked them carefully, L'Aiglon," he said as at last he laid down both pieces of the paper. "These French specifications and figures that floored you, represent the ideal mule in bulk and these United States figures promise the same multitude in scrub. I thought as much. You just run in there to Bill with them and then forget you ever saw them, and we'll be on our way to the girls in ten minutes. Bobby, I mean it when I say that men in your and my positions of trust just forget facts and figures the minute we get out of sight of our chiefs. And we forget the chiefs too, believe me. Now run along and come out to the car on the same trot."

"Is it of honor not to tell to the Gouverneur Faulkner that you assisted me in this task, my Buzz?" I asked of him with anxiety.

"No need to tell him - it's all in the same office and will come to me for filing. Don't say anything that will bring on talk that keeps us from Sue and the gang. Just run!" With which advice my kind Buzz disappeared through the door into the office of my Uncle, the General Robert, as I softly opened the door of the room of the Gouverneur Faulkner and entered into his presence. And in that presence I found also my Uncle, the General Robert, in a very grave consultation with the Gouverneur Faulkner.

"The papers completed, Your Excellency," I said in a very low and meek tone of my voice as I laid the papers beside him on the table and prepared to take the running departure that my Buzz had commanded of me.

"Bless my soul, are you here and at work, young man? I thought you were asleep after all that gallivanting, and was just preparing to blow you up out of bed over the telephone," exclaimed my Uncle, the General Robert, with great fierceness of manner but also a great pleasure of eyes at the sight of me in the character of such a nice Secretary to the Gouverneur of Harpeth.

"Robert arrived five minutes after I did and ten minutes before you came into the building, General," said that Gouverneur Faulkner, with a twinkle of great enjoyment in his eyes. "He's done a day's work before we have begun. Will you have your luncheon sent up from the restaurant with ours, Robert? Just order the usual things for us and any kind of frills you care for. Shall I say snails?"

"I thank Your Excellency deeply but I am engaged that I luncheon and dance with Mr. Buzz Clendenning in his club in the country if I may be given permission to go," I answered as I laid my fingers with affection on the arm of my Uncle, the General Robert, as I stood beside him.

"Nonsense, sir! You'll not join those jackanapes in their gambols during business hours. Order yourself up a slice of pie and a glass of buttermilk along with mine and sit down here to listen to matters of business by which you can profit. Luncheon and dancing! No, pie and business, I say, pie and business!" And the fierceness of my Uncle, the General Robert, made me retire several feet away from him in astonishment and in the direction of the Gouverneur Faulkner.

"Now, General, don't tie the boy down to pie and the company of two musty old gentlemen like ourselves. He's earned a dance. You may go, Robert, and I wish - I wish my heels were light enough to go with yours," that kind Gouverneur said in my behalf.

"Light heels, light head! And I say he shall -" And another explosion of fierceness was about to arrive from my Uncle, the General Robert, when I said with great and real humility:

"It will be my great pleasure to sit at the feet of you

and His Excellency, which are not light for dancing, my Uncle Robert, and eat a large piece of pie and also milk." I spoke with a sincerity, for suddenly I knew that there would be nothing at that dance of girls in the club of my Buzz that I would so desire as to sit near to that Gouverneur Faulkner, in whose eyes came that sadness when he spoke of the dance for which he had not the light feet, and eat with him and my Uncle, the General Robert, a piece of that American pie of which I had heard my father speak many times.

"Why, he means it, General," said the Gouverneur Faulkner with a great softness in his eyes that answered the affection that was in mine that pleaded for the pie and a place at his side. "Run, youngster, run, before the General says another word. You are dismissed. Go!" And with a great laugh the Gouverneur Faulkner rose, put his arm around my shoulder and put me out of that room before my Uncle, the General Robert, could begin any more words of remonstrance. And I ran away from that door to my Buzz in the waiting car with both light and reluctant feet.

The two hours that I spent with my Buzz at his club in the country with what he called in front of their very faces, bunches of calico, passed with such a rapidity that I felt I must grasp each minute and remonstrate with them for their fleetness. That Mademoiselle Sue was even much more lovely in her gray costume of golf with a tie the color of the one worn by my Buzz, than she had been in her chiffon of the dinner dance, and the beautiful Belle was much the same, with an added gayety and charm, while I discovered a very sweet Kate Keith and a Mildred Summers who was not of a great beauty but of many interesting remarks which induced much laughing. With them were that Miles Menefee whom my Buzz had recommended to me, and also several young gentlemen of America whom I liked exceedingly. One Mr. Phillips Taylor took me by my heart with a great force when, as we were all seated on the steps of the wide porch eating the promised sandwich and consuming breath for another dance in a very few minutes, he said to me:

"Say, Mr. Robert Carruthers, my mater wants to see you over in the east card room directly. She says she had it on with your father in their dancing school days and it was only by the intervention of some sort of love ruckus that you and I are not brothers or maybe what would be worse, brother and sister. If that had happened you would have had to be it. I wouldn't. But that's not our quarrel."

"You couldn't have been a woman unless you had received a much better finishing polish before being sent to bless the earth, Phil, dear," said that funny Mademoiselle Mildred Summers, and that Mr. Phillips Taylor returned the insult by lifting her off of her feet and gliding her halfway across the porch verandah in the beginning of one tango dance to the music that was again to be heard from the hall within the building.

"Mildred and Phil fight like aborigines, and their love for combat will lead to matrimony in their early youth if they are not reconciled to each other soon," said lovely Sue as she fitted herself into my arms for our tango.

"After this dance with you will you lead me to that Madam Taylor, the friend of my father, beautiful Sue?" I asked of her. "It makes happy my heart to see one who loved him." And as I spoke, the longing for my father that will ever be in my heart made a sadness in my voice and a dimness in my eyes.

"I think everybody loved him just as we are all beginning to - to like you, Bobby dear," said that sweet girl as she smiled up at me in a way that sent the dimness in my eyes back to my heart.

"I am very grateful that you like me, lovely Sue," I said with great humility. "I will endeavor to win and deserve more and more of that liking, until it is with me as if I had been born in a house near to yours, as is the case with my dear Buzz and also that funny Mildred."

"I couldn't like you any better, Bobby, if you had torn the hair off of my doll's head or broken my slate a dozen times," she laughed at me again as we slid together the last slide in the dance. "Now come over and be introduced to Mrs. Taylor. You have only a few minutes, for you and Buzz must both be back at the Capitol at two. I feel in honor bound to the State to send you both back on time." And while she spoke she led me across the hall of the clubhouse and into a room full of ladies, who sat at card tables consuming very beautiful food while also preparing to resume playing the cards.

CHAPTER XII

THE BEAUTIFUL MADAM WHITWORTH

Sue then made for me many introductions and all of those lovely *grande dames* gave to me affectionate welcomes. Some of them I had encountered at the dance of the Gouverneur Faulkner and all of them had smiles for me.

"Why, boy, you are Henry's very self come back to us after all these years - only with a lot of added deviltry in the way of French beauty," said that Madam Taylor, who was very stately, with white hair and a very young countenance of sweetness. "The daredevil - it was like him to send you back to us as - as revenge," she added with something that almost seemed like anger under the sweetness of her voice.

"It is what my father always named me, Madam, the 'daredevil,' and will you not accept me for your cherishing?" I spoke those words to her from an impulse that I could not understand but I saw them soothe a hurt in her eyes as she laughed and kissed my cheek as I raised my head from kissing her jeweled hand.

"Yes," she answered me softly.

"Come on, L'Aiglon; it's time to beat it. We are late and Sue is beginning to shoo," called my Buzz from the door of the card room. "We are coming home with Phil for supper to-night, Mrs. Taylor, and the Prince wants an introduction to your custard pie. Yes'm, seven sharp! Come on, Bob!"

"My Buzz," I said to that Mr. Buzz Clendenning as he raced the slim car through the country and the city up to the Capitol hill, "you give to me a life of much joy in only a few days. I would that it could so continue."

"It just will until we are jolly old boys with long white beards and canes, Bobby," he answered me with an affectionate grin as we rounded a corner on two wheels of the car. "Say, let's get out of this politics soon, go in for selling timber lands, marry two of the calicoes and found families. We'll call the firm Carruthers and Clendenning and I choose Sue. You can decide about your dame later."

Suddenly something very cold and dead was there in place of my heart that had danced with happiness. What should I do at that time of disclosing myself as one large lie to all of these kind friends who were giving me affection on the account of my honored father and Uncle, the General Robert? That daredevil in me had led me into this dishonor, with the excuse, it is true, of fear that the wicked Uncle would not have mended the hip of small Pierre if I did not obey his summons as a nephew. And now I must stay to be of service to him and to the Gouverneur Faulkner but also to be more involved in that lie and to accept more confidence and affection with thievery.

"I cannot sell the lands of timber with you, my Buzz," I

made answer to him quickly and with fierceness. "As soon as this business of the mules is settled and my Uncle, the General Robert, no longer requires my services, I must return and go into the trenches of France." And I felt as I spoke that my fate was decided, and a great calmness came over me. "Then I'll go with you," answered me that Buzz with a look of the steadfast affection which might have grown with years of comradeship. "I'll go and fight for France with you if you'll come back and build an American family alongside of mine. Jump out - we are fifteen minutes late - and watch the General scalp me. Come in through his office and take a part of it, will you?"

Even in the very short time which I had known my Uncle, the General Robert, I had discovered that the times at which could be anticipated explosions, none came, and also the reverse of that fact. When my Buzz and I entered his office he very hastily concealed a book that had some variety of richly colored pictures in it in his desk and smiled with a wink of the eye at my Buzz. Later I should know about that book to my great joy.

"Here's a letter for you, Robert, and go get to your knitting with Governor Bill," he said to me with kindness in his smile as he handed me a large letter and motioned me from the room into the small anteroom that I now knew to be the place assigned to my Buzz and me when not wanted in the offices of my Uncle, the General Robert, or the Gouverneur Faulkner. I made a low bow to my Uncle, the General Robert, and also to Monsieur the Bumble Bee and departed thence.

On seating myself at my table to await the bell of the Gouverneur Faulkner, without which ringing my Buzz had instructed me I must never on pain of extinction as a secretary enter His Excellency's office, I opened that letter and began to read with difficulty a letter of a few words from my wee Pierre, now in the hospital of that kind Doctor Burns. I read not more than one sentence when I leaped to my feet with a cry of joy and my heart beat very high with happiness. To whom should I turn to tell of that happiness? I did not pause to answer that question in my heart but I quickly opened the door of the august Gouverneur of Harpeth and presented myself to him in a disobedience of strict orders. And then what befell me?

Seated at his desk was that great and good man, with his head bowed upon his hands; and at my entrance he raised that head with an alarm. I could see that his face was heavy and sad with deep pondering and I was instantly thrown into mortification that I had so interrupted him. I faltered there beside him and found halting words to exclaim:

"Oh, it is a pardon I ask Your Excellency for intruding into your door, but it is that my small Pierre has stood upon two feet for perhaps a whole minute in the hospital of that good Dr. Burns and I must run to tell you of my joy. Is it quite possible now that Pierre will no longer be for life crooked in the back?" And as I spoke I held out to him the letter upon which tears were dripping and one of my hands I clasped trembling at my breast that shook under that stylish cheviot bag of a coat I had that morning put upon me for the first time. And did that great Gouverneur Faulkner repulse his wicked secretary? He did not.

"God bless you, youngster! Of course you run right to tell me when a big thing like that happens. Sure that back will be all straight in no time and we'll have the little maid down, running in and out at her will in just a few months," and as he spoke that Gouverneur Faulkner came to my side and took the hand that held the tear-besprinkled letter and also drew the one from my breast into his own two large and warm ones. "I've been hearing people's troubles for what seems like an eternity, boy, but not a single son-of-a-gun has run to me with his joy until you have. Here, use one corner of my handkerchief while I use the other," and as he spoke that very large and broad-shouldered man released one of my hands, dabbed his own eyes that were sparkling with perhaps a tear, and then handed that handkerchief to me.

And those tears of both of us ended in a large laugh.

"It is my habit that I shed tears when in joy," I said with apology, as I returned that large white hand-kerchief to that Gouverneur Faulkner.

"Mind you don't tell anybody that Governor Bill Faulkner does the same thing," he answered with a laugh.

"I have a feeling that is of longing to rush to small Pierre and to prostrate myself at the feet of that good Doctor," I said as again the great joy of that news rushed upon me.

"No, boy, not right now," answered that great Gouverneur Faulkner as he turned and laid a large warm hand on each of my shoulders. "The crisis is at hand and I need you here for a little time. I can't explain it, but - but you seem to feed - feed my faith in myself. In just a few days I've grown to depend on you to - to -. You ridiculous boy, you, with your storms and joy sunbursts, get out of here and tell Cato to send Mr. Whitworth and Mr. Brown into my office immediately." And with a laugh and a shake of me away from his side, the Gouverneur Faulkner picked up the two long sheets of paper which had been of so much labor to my Buzz and me and began to scowl back of his black, white-tipped eyebrows over them. I departed with great rapidity.

Then with much more calmness I told the great news of the back of Pierre to my Uncle, the General Robert.

"That's fine - now we can give her away without any trouble. I knew Burns could do the trick. It's a bargain at two thousand dollars to get a girl in the shape to give away. She could give us no end of bother if we had to keep her. Go find that flea, Clendenning, and tell him to come to me immediately; I think he is buzzing in the telephone closet to that Susan. And you go get busy yourself to earn your salary from the State of Harpeth. Telegraph twenty dollars to that fool nurse to buy a doll for the girl. Now go!" That was the way that my Uncle, the General Robert, received my news of the improved health of the back of small Pierre, and with my two eyes I shed a few secret tears that did roll down into my mouth which was broad from a laugh as I went in search of my Buzz.

"Bully, old top," said my Bumble Bee as I imparted also my joy to him. "Say, if that kid is eight years old and is going to walk all right, we must see to it that she starts in with a good dancing teacher as soon as she can spin around. We want to make a real winner out of her."

"I do love you, my Buzz," I answered to him as I clung with both my hands to his arm across my shoulder.

"That's all right. Prince, but don't talk about it," he answered me with a laugh and a shake.

"And, say, let's get to work, because at about four o'clock I'll have something that'll give you a start."

"Oh, but, my Buzz, at four o'clock I must go for tea to the home of beautiful Madam Whitworth."

"Whe-ee-uh!" whistled my Buzz as he looked at me from the top of my head to the toe of my shoe.

"It would give me a much greater pleasure to be startled by you, my Buzz, but this is a promise I did make the last evening," I pleaded to him.

"Go ahead, sport, but accept it from me that Madam Pat is the genuine and original pump; so don't let her empty you. Do you want me to come by and extract you at about fifteen to five? I'm sorry, but I really must have a business interview with you before six." And my Buzz's eyes twinkled with something that was of a great pleasure to him I could observe.

"It would be of more pleasure to me if you came at the half of five, my Buzz," I made a hurry to assure him, for I had a great dread of all of the falsehoods I was to say to that Madam Whitworth that afternoon for the purpose of extracting perhaps a little wicked truth from her to help in the defense of my Gouverneur Faulkner.

"I'm on," answered my Buzz promptly. "Beat it! I hear the old boy growling." And he disappeared behind the door of my Uncle, the General Robert. I went to the duty of assuring the nice gentleman in very rough clothing that the Gouverneur would in the morning read the paper on the subject of making a long road past his property in good condition by a vote, and I was of a very great success in my efforts, the good Cato assured me.

"You's got a fine oiled tongue tied in the middle and loose at both ends, honey. Yo' father had the same," he assured me as he handed me my hat and walking cane at the hour of four, which ended my duties for the day. Roberta, Marquise of Grez and Bye, did so long to go into that room of the Gouverneur Faulkner and receive upon her hand one nice kiss of good night from him, but Mr. Robert Carruthers walked down from the Capitol and only paused to lift for a little second his very handsome hat towards the window of His Excellency's room high up above.

And the encounter with the beautiful Madam Whitworth was much worse than I had thought that it would be, though also it was of a very interesting excitement. She had made armaments for the encounter in the shape of a very lovely tea apparel of an increditable thinness to be used for covering, a little low fire in the golden grate, and curtains of rose to throw somewhat of glow over the situation. Immediately I was seated beside her on a small divan upon which there was room for only one and a half persons, and my stupidity was called into vigorous action.

"I suppose you have spent the day in translating a lot of those long and tiresome French documents for the General and the Governor. Thank goodness, that is no longer my task," she remarked as she tipped the cognac bottle over my tea and handed the cup to me.

"It is of a great fatigue to work upon a matter that one does not at all understand," I answered her as I sipped at that tea of a very disagreeable taste because of the cognac.

"Did they give you the two sets of specifications to compare?" she asked of me with not much of interest apparent in her manner, though her hand shook as she poured for herself a very small cup of tea, which was then filled complete with the cognac.

"*Helas*," I answered with a sigh. "And it is impossible for me to add more figures to each other than my fingers will allow. I cannot even use my toes."

"Then he didn't get them ready for the conference this afternoon?" she demanded with a great illumination of joy in her face.

"Oh, indeed, I handed them back completed to His Excellency in a short space of time. Is not one mule like to another exactly, and why should a paper make them different?" I questioned with deceit of stupidity.

"You are a dear boy," laughed that Madam Whitworth. "Of course those specifications agree, for I worked a whole day over them; and I'm glad you didn't tire your eyes out with them. You know you are really a very beautiful creature and I think I'll kiss you just once, purely for the pleasure of it." And I thereupon received a kiss upon my lips from the curled flower which was the mouth of that beautiful Madam Whitworth.

"Is it that the stupid Gouverneur Faulkner must very

soon sign that paper that sends the many strong mules to carry food to the soldiers of France fighting in the trenches?" I asked of her as I made her comfortable in the hollow of my arm.

"If he doesn't sign them in a very few days the deal is all off," she answered me. "Jeff has got his capital to put up from some Northern men who are - are restless and - and suspicious. It must go through and immediately."

"Then it must be accomplished immediately," I answered her with decision.

"The agent of the French Government will be here on Tuesday and all of these preliminary papers must be signed before he can close the matter up finally. I hope that the conference over those specifications this afternoon will be the last. Are you sure you discovered no flaw over which the old General or the big stupid Governor can haggle?"

"I discovered not a flaw," I answered her with a great positiveness. "Do you say that it is soon that those representatives of my government come to make a last signing of the papers about the excellent mules to be sent from the great State of Harpeth to France who is at a war of death? I had not heard of the nearness of the visit at the Capitol."

"They don't know it - that is, Governor Faulkner does, but has told only me. He sees things my way but of - of course, he has to keep his councils from his Secretary of State for the time being. And I'm telling you all about it, because - because it is for France we plot and because I - this is the way to say it." And with those wicked words, which involved the honor of the great Gouverneur Faulkner, she pressed her body close to mine and her lips upon my mouth.

For that caress of that wicked woman I had not sufficient endurance and I pushed her from me with roughness and sprang to my feet.

"It is not true, Madam Whitworth, that -" I was exclaiming when I caught myself in the midst of my own betrayal, just as I was about to be shown into a plot which it was of much value to know. And as my words ceased I stood and trembled before her wickedness.

"Do you know, Mr. Robert Carruthers, I do not entirely understand you," she said with a great and beautiful calmness as she lighted a cigarette and looked at me trembling before her. "You are a very bold young cavalier but you have the shrinking nature of - shall I say? - a French - *girl!*"

As she spoke those words, which began in sarcasm but ended in a queer uncertain tone of suspicion, as if she had blundered on a reason to soothe her vanity for the recoil of my lips from hers, an ugly gleam shot from under her lowered lashes.

"I am the son of the house of Carruthers as well as of Grez and Bye, beautiful Madam, and I cannot endure that you put upon my very good Uncle, the General Carruthers, an unfriendliness to France," I exclaimed with a quickness of my brain that I had not before discovered. "On points of honor I have that sensitiveness that you say to be - be of a woman."

"Oh, my darling boy, I didn't mean to hurt you about that absurd old feud of -" And as she spoke the beautiful Madam Patricia rose and came upon me with outstretched arms for another abhorred embrace, which it was to my good fortune to have interrupted. But I had a fear of that suspicion I had seen flashed into her mind even though lulled by my fine assumption of the attitude of a man of honor.

"Lovely and beautiful Madam," I made a beginning to say, when -

"Oh, yes, Mr. Carruthers is here, for I have an appointment to call for him," an interruption came in the voice of my Buzz in remonstrance with the black maid of Madam Whitworth in the hall of her house.

"Come in, Buzz, dear," called that beautiful Madam Whitworth as in one small instant she changed both her position with arms on my shoulder and her countenance of anger and anxiety. She was a very wise and beautiful and much experienced woman, was that Madam Whitworth, but she had given to me, unlessoned as I was in the art of politics, the fact that I most wanted: that the two papers containing the specifications concerning the mules had been mistranslated by her.

"Put a shawl around you, Madam Pat, and come out here to the street a minute to see what is going to happen to the Prince of Carruthers," said my rescuer as he inserted his head into the room for one little minute and beckoned us to follow him.

And what did I find out there upon that street?

CHAPTER XIII

BROTHERS BY BLOODSHED

I then experienced a surprise that gave to me a very great pleasure and which made my heart to expand until it almost burst the restraint of that towel of the bath under the bag of my brown cheviot coat. Before the door of the house of the beautiful Madam Whitworth stood the gray racing car of my Buzz, and before it stood a slim car of a similar make, only it was of the darkest amethyst that seemed to be almost a black, while behind it stood one of equal if not superior elegance of shape which had the beautiful blackness of jet. That was not all! Across the street stood also a car of a golden brown and to the front of it one of the red of a very dark cherry.

"There you are," said my Buzz with a wave of his hand. "Pick one, with the compliments of the General. I think the amethyst is a jewel."

"Oh, it is not possible to me to accept a present of such delight from my good Uncle, the General Robert. I must go to him and say that I am not worthy!" I exclaimed with a large faltering in my voice.

"All right; just jump into the one you like best and drive on down to the Old Hickory Club and say it to him. Sorry that you can't come along, Mrs. Pat, but that glad rag you've got on is too great a beauty with which to appear in public. Better take it into the house before you catch a cold in this breeze."

"Yes, I must run in," answered Madam Whitworth with a slight shivering in her gown of great thinness. "They are perfectly wonderful, boy, and I say choose the brown darling."

"Governor Bill picked the cherry from the catalogue for us day before yesterday, but I think the amethyst has got it beat," answered my Buzz as he started towards his own car. "Jump into your choice and lead me on down to hear you refuse it to old Forty-Two Centimeter."

Then without further remark, I followed him down the steps and got into that car which was the color of the heart of the cherry and I raced that Mr. Bumble Bee through the city of Hayesville in a manner which put to flight a large population thereof. I had not had my hands on the wheel of a racing car for the many months since my father in his had left the small Pierre and Nannette and me weeping on the terrace of the Chateau de Grez when he went to the battlefield of the Marne, and I drove with all of that accumulated fury within me. And I could see that my Buzz enjoyed it as much as did I, though in his face was a great fear as several very large policemen waved their hands at us and then savagely transcribed the numbers of his car in books from their pockets when we whirled on with refusal to stop and listen to their remarks.

And this is what my Uncle, the General Robert, answered to me as I told him of my unworthiness of his gift of the most beautiful cherry car:

"That is a just return for your consideration for me in being born a boy, and I hope you'll break the necks of about two dozen young females in this town before the week's out. Begin on that baggage, Susan, right away." And as he spoke, my Uncle, the General Robert, came down the steps of the great Club of Old Hickory with the Gouverneur Faulkner and stood beside my Cherry with me.

"He's no better man than I, General, and I've been trying it all year," answered my Buzz with one of those delectable grinnings upon his face.

"Indeed, my much loved Uncle Robert, it is impossible that I accept your gift in gratitude that I am not a woman, because for the good reason - " and my honor was about to rise up in arms and betray the daredevil and her schemes within me when that good and most beloved Gouverneur Faulkner interrupted me by stepping into the Cherry beside me with a laugh.

"Thank you, General; this is just what I need in all of my business with Robert. We'll be back in time to dine with you at seven here at the Club. Go out to the West End, Robert." And with his hand on the spark he started the Cherry, and I was forced to sweep away from my Buzz and my Uncle, the General Robert, into the traffic and away from the Club of Old Hickory, which is named for a very great general of America and is a club of much fashion and some bad behavior, my Buzz has said to me.

"I really didn't mean to kidnap you and the car, youngster, but I've had a pain under my left pocket all day, and I have got to operate on it. A sudden impulse told me that it would be easier if I took you with me to - to sort of stand by," said my beautiful Gouverneur Faulkner in a grave tone of voice as I whirled him out the broad avenue that led to the west end of the city.

"Oh, my Gouverneur Faulkner, is it that you are ill, perhaps to die by a knife?" I exclaimed and for a second I let that wild Cherry run in a very dangerous manner almost upon another large car in the act of turning into the street.

"No, not that, Robert," he answered me quickly and he laid his hand on my arm beside him for an instant as if to give a steadiness to me. "I want you to take me out to the State Prison. I want to talk face to face with a man who killed his own brother, in cold blood, it is said. A pretty powerful influence is at me day and night for a reprieve and I - I don't know what to do about it. It is a difficult case. If I went in my official capacity to see the man it might give his friends undue hopes; and suddenly I felt that I could run away from the whole bunch at this hour of the day and see the man himself without anybody's knowing it save the superintendent of the prison and myself. You don't count, because in this case you are myself."

"Always I would be yourself to you, my reverenced Gouverneur Faulkner," I made reply to him as I raised my eyes to his deep ones that smiled down into them.

"I wonder if that is as good as it sounds, boy," asked my Gouverneur Faulkner gently, as he looked down at me with both a laugh and a sadness influencing the smile of his mouth. "Sometimes I badly need two of myself. They are at me from waking to sleeping and I often feel cut into little bits and I can't even say so. In fact, youngster, I'm squealing to you more than I've let myself do since I became the chief executive of this State of Harpeth. Now, turn off into this road and go straight ahead. The prison is about a mile back there at the foot of that hill."

"I - like those squeals," I answered to his smile as I put my Cherry against the spring wind and raced down that long road at a great speed that prevented any more conversation at that moment. My pride bade me show to that Gouverneur of Harpeth what good driving in a fine car I was able to accomplish.

Therefore it was not many minutes before we stood within the doors of that very grim and terrible home of the human beings who have sinned with a great crime. I know that I am never to forget that hour and am to carry forever the wound that it inflicted upon my heart as I walked through the dimness and grayness and stillness of that dark house.

At last, with many unlockings of heavy doors by the director of that prison, we stood in a room that was as a cage in which to keep the human animal that crouched down upon a hard bed in one of its corners and leaned a head shaved bare of any hair upon a very thin and white hand.

"Leave me, Superintendent, for a few minutes. The young man will stay by the door to let you know when I want you," said that Gouverneur Faulkner to the superintendent, who nodded and left the room as I took a position over beside the heavy iron bars that swung together after him.

"My man," said the Gouverneur Faulkner in a voice that was so gentle as that which a mother uses to a child in severe illness, "I want you to let me sit down on your cot beside you and talk to you about your trouble."

"Got nothing to say, parson. I done it and I want to swing as quick as the law sends me," answered the poor human from behind his hands without even raising his bowed head.

"I am not a minister, and I've come to talk to you because some of your neighbors and friends think that there may be a reason why you should not be hanged for the death of your brother. It is my duty to help them keep you from the penalty of the law, which you may not deserve even if you desire it. Can you tell me your story as man to man, with the hope that it will help you to a reprieve?" And as he spoke I observed a tone of command come into the voice of my Gouverneur Faulkner, that was as clear and beautiful as the call of the bugle to men for a battle.

"I done what I had to and I'm ready to die for it. I've got nothing to say," answered the man with still more of the determination of misery in his voice. "My neighbors don't know nothing about it and I don't want 'em to. Just let them keep quiet and let it all die when the State swings me."

"So there is some secret about the matter that you are willing to die to keep, is there?" asked the Gouverneur Faulkner with a quickness of command in his voice. "What had your brother done to Mary Brown that you killed him for doing?"

"Damn you, what's that to you?" snarled the man as he sprang up from beside the Gouverneur and leaned, crouched and panting, against the bars of the cage in which the three of us were inclosed. "Who are you anyway? My State has said I was to swing for killing him and there's no more to question about it."

"I am the Governor of your State," answered that Gouverneur Faulkner as he rose and stood tall and commanding before the poor human being who was cowering as a dog that had felt the lash of a whip. "You are my son because you are a son of the State of Harpeth, and as a representative of that State I am going to exercise my guardianship and if possible prevent the State from the crime of taking your life if you do not deserve punishment."

"I'm condemned by the laws of the State. You can't go back on that, Governor or no Governor," made answer the man, with a panting of misery in his voice.

"As you know, there are certain unwritten laws which have more influence in some cases as to the guilt of a murderer than any on the statute books," said the Gouverneur Faulkner with a very great slowness, so that the poor human dog might comprehend him. "If you killed your brother to save - save Mary Brown from worse than death, then you have not the right to demand execution from your State to shelter her from publicity when she is no longer in danger of anything worse. Did you get to her in time to save her or -"
"Yes, good God, I did and I had - damn you, now I'll have to kill you for getting words out of me that all the lawyers have tried to make me say all this time," and with the oath and a snarl the man made a lunge at my Gouverneur Faulkner with something keen and shining

that he had drawn from the top of his coarse boot. But that poor human being of the prison was not of enough quickness to do the killing of his desire in the face of Roberta, Marquise of Grez and Bye, who had twice with her foil pricked the red cloth heart of the young Count de Couertoir, the best swordsman of France, in gay combat in the great hall of the old Chateau de Grez. With my walking cane of a young gentleman of American fashion, which I had taken with me to call upon the beautiful Madam Whitworth before my Cherry had befallen me as a gift, and which I had without thought brought into that prison with me, I parried the blow of the knife at my beloved Gouverneur Faulkner, but not in such a manner as to prevent a glancing of that knife, which inflicted a scratch of considerable depth upon my forearm under its sleeve of brown cheviot.

"My God, boy!" exclaimed that Gouverneur Faulkner as he caught the knife from the floor where it had fallen from the hand of the poor man who had sunk down on the cot, trembling and panting. "Two inches to the left and a little more force and the knife would have stuck in your heart."

"Is it not better my heart than yours, my great Gouverneur Faulkner? And behold it is the heart of neither and only a small scratch upon my humble arm, which will not even prevent the driving of that new Cherry car," I answered him as I put that arm behind me and pressed it close in its sleeve of brown cheviot so that there would be no drippings of blood.

"I didn't go to hurt the young gentleman nor you either, Governor," said the man from the cot as he sobbed and buried his head in his arms. "I was always a good man and now I -"

"Don't say another word, Timms," interrupted my Gouverneur Faulkner in a voice that was as gentle as that father of State which he had said himself to be to Timms. "Nobody will know of this, for your sake. I was - was baiting you. I know what I want to know now and you'll not hang on the sixteenth. The State will try you again. Call the superintendent, Robert."

"Don't say nothing to hurt Mary, Governor. Jest let me hang and I won't never care what -" the poor human began to plead.

"I'll look after Mary - and you too, Timms. I'll see to it that -" my Gouverneur Faulkner was answering the trembling plea for his mercy when the superintendent came in and unlocked the cage.

"Don't let him know of the - accident, youngster," whispered the Gouverneur Faulkner to me, and in a very few minutes we were out of that prison into the Cherry car, and whirling with great rapidity down the country road with its tall trees upon both sides.

"Stop, Robert," commanded His Excellency as we came under a large group of very old trees which made a thick shelter of their green leaves as they leaned together over the stone wall that bordered the side of the road. "Now let me see just what did happen to that arm which came between poor Timms' sharpened case knife and my life. We are out of sight of the prison now. It would have all been up with Timms if that attack upon me had been discovered. Your pluck will have saved Timms, if he's saved, as well as your Governor. Here, turn towards me and let me see that arm." And as he spoke, my Gouverneur Faulkner put his arm across my shoulder and turned me towards him so that he could put his right hand on the sleeve of that cheviot bag in which was a long slash from the knife and which was now wet with my blood.

"I very much fear my beloved brown cheviot, which I have worn only a few times, is now dead; and how will I find another for my need!" I exclaimed with a great alarm when I saw that that knife had thus devastated my good clothing of which I had not many and for the procuring of which I was many thousand miles from my good friend and tailor in New York. If I sought another suit in the city of Hayesville might there not be dangers of discoveries in the adjustment thereof? "Is it not a vexation?" I asked as the Gouverneur Faulkner attempted to push back that murdered sleeve from my forearm.

"In the language of my friend Buzz, you are one sport, Robert. Shell out of that coat immediately. I want to see just how much of a scratch that is and I can't get the sleeve up high enough," commanded my Gouverneur Faulkner. The tone of his voice was the same he had used to me in commanding that I take his mail to his nice lady stenographer, but his face was very white and his hand that he laid upon the collar of my coat for assisting me to lay it aside trembled with a great degree of violence.

"Indeed, my Gouverneur Faulkner, it is but a scratch and -"

"Get out of that coat!"

"But -"

"Off with that coat, Robert!" he commanded me, and before I could make resistance, my coat was almost completely off of me by his aid and I was obliged to let it slip into his hands. He laid it on the back of the seat behind him, and with hands that were as gentle as those of old Nannette when dealing with one of my injuries of a great number in childhood, he rolled up the sleeve of my nice white shirt with the brown strip of coloring in accord with that beloved and regretted cheviot, and bared my forearm, which was very strong and white but which also appeared to me to be dangerously rounded for his gaze. I was glad that that arm was covered with a nice gore which had come from the long slit but which had now well-nigh ceased to run from me, so that he could not observe that it was of such a feminine mould.

"Yes, just a deep scratch that I can fix all right myself in my own bathroom when we get back to the Mansion in time for dinner with the General by seven-thirty, I hope," said my beloved Gouverneur as he helped me again to assume the ruined garment of cheviot. "I was born in the mountains of the State of Harpeth, boy, where when one man sheds his blood for the life of another, that other is said to be under bond to his rescuer and that means a tie closer than the ordinary one of brother by birth. I acknowledge the bond to you for all time, little brother. Now drive on quickly to the Mansion before we are in danger of being late for dinner with the General. It will take me some few minutes to get you out of that shirt and into your dinner coat. I'll send for it and you can dress with me."

"Oh, no, my beloved Gouverneur Faulkner; I must go immediately to home and there make myself presentable for a dinner of some very wonderful pie that my

Buzz demanded of that very lovely Madam Taylor in my honor. That nice black lady, Kizzie, will with joy attend on this scratch upon my arm, assisted by my good Bonbon," I exclaimed with great alarm for fear that that very strong mind of my Gouverneur would command me to make my toilet in his company in the Mansion. "Please do not command me that I shall not so do."

"Of course, youngster, go to your frolic with the rest of the babes and sucklings, only remember that I always like to have you with me, but - never command you when it is not your pleasure," answered that Gouverneur Faulkner to me with gentleness.

"It is always my pleasure to be with you, my Gouverneur, and I do like that you command me," I said to him in answer to that gentleness that had something of a sad longing in it - for that custard pie of Madam Taylor, I suppose, of which he had probably heard famous mention, but which I would have believed to have been a longing for Roberta, Marquise of Grez and Bye, if I had heard it so spoken, with an English or Russian or French accent, to me in a robe of tulle or sheer linen. "And may I not return immediately after that supper to that Club of Old Hickory for conversation with you and my Uncle, the General Robert?" I asked with eagerness.

"Boy, by the time you have eaten that fatted pie at the Taylors' and danced at least a portion of it off of your system I'll be - be burning the midnight oil going over the papers in the case of Timms. I want to weigh all the testimony carefully in the case given in Court about his own and his brother's relations with the woman Mary Brown. As long as I am the Governor of the State of

Harpeth, no honest man is going to swing for protecting a good woman from the outrages of a brute. And yet Timms confessed the crime and denied the motive. Cross-examining failed to get the statement from the woman that would justify my reprieving or pardoning him. I cannot even seem to dishonor the proceedings of the courts of the State and, boy, I'm just plain - up - against - it. Here we are at my own side door. Good night, and make a lightning toilet if you want to get to that pie on time. Good night, again!" And with those words, which explained his very deep trouble to me, my Gouverneur Faulkner descended from the seat beside me in the Cherry to the pavement beside his Mansion and bade me hurry from him.

CHAPTER XIV

TO BEAR MEN AND TO SAVE THEM

In going I turned and looked back at him to see that he was standing looking after me with a very great weariness in the manner of the drooping of his shoulders and the sadness of his face.

"Roberta," I said to myself, "a woman who so reverences and regards a man as you do that Gouverneur Faulkner will find a way to help him so that he shall not suffer as he does in regard to not knowing with surety the reason of that Mr. Timms' making a murder upon his brother. What is it that you shall do?"

And to that question to myself I found an answer in only two short hours while partaking of the very famous custard pie at the table of that very lovely Madam Taylor.

All of those very gay and nice "babes and sucklings" which the Gouverneur Faulkner had mentioned, were with me at the table of Madam Taylor with very much laughter and merriment, also much conversation. And in that conversation were very many jokes upon my Buzz because he had been transported to the Capitol by my Uncle, the General Robert, and given hard labor until almost the time to arrive for that nice supper, which he was eating with much hunger. On account of lateness he had not been able to come to the house of lovely Sue to escort her with him to the home of Madam Taylor. That Sue with pretended haughtiness was looking very high above the head of the humble Buzz.

"Well, it's not my fault that Timms up and biffed his brother into eternity all for buzzing pretty Mary Brown, and I don't see why I had to be rung in to sort out of a million sheets of trial evidence the lies he told about it, for poor old Governor Bill to moil over all night. I say when a man wants to be hung as badly as that, he ought to get what he's crying for, and not butt in on a perfectly innocent man's afternoon fox trot," was that Mr. Buzz Clendenning's wailing to all of the company. "Look the other way, Sue, so as not to turn this muffin cold until I get it buttered."

"I told my washwoman, who is Mary's sister, that Mary ought to be made to tell just what did happen and then it could all be arranged so that the poor man could be saved to her. I think it is hard on Mary to lose both lovers," said that very intelligent Mildred Summers.

"They live just over beyond our back gate. Suppose we all go and put it up to the attractive Mary to speak up and keep Buzz from the danger of overwork a second time," said that nice young Mr. Taylor with what I considered a great intelligence but which caused much laughter.

And at that suggestion which caused the much merriment, that daredevil within Roberta, Marquise of Grez and Bye , again arose and commanded me to attention.

"Go, Robert Carruthers, and obtain that paper of statement from that Mary, so that your chief, that good Gouverneur Faulkner, does not work in the night which is for rest, and that your beloved Buzz may not again have to work in his afternoon which is for dancing. Go and find that Mary as soon as this dinner is at an end."

And what was it possible for me to do but to answer the command of the daredevil person within me? All of which I did. I made excuse of myself on account of a lie which involved my attendance on my Uncle, the General Robert, and departed after I had had but one nice slide with the lovely Sue, but had obtained a promise of one from Mademoiselle Belle if I found it possible to return by the hour of ten o'clock.

After many inquiries at the back of the house of Madam Taylor in small streets I was at last led to the home of the Mary Brown. All was dark within the very small house, but upon the steps, in the light from the moon and also a street arc, sat the person that a man, of whom I had asked guidance, said to be the woman whom I sought. She rested her head in her hands as had done that poor human in the cage in that State Prison and from her I heard the sounds of slow weeping.

"What is it that I shall say to her?" I asked of myself. And then suddenly something answered from within me from the same place that had arisen that knowledge to spring in between my Gouverneur Faulkner and the bright knife I had not even seen. That place is located in the heart of Roberta, Marquise of Grez and Bye, and not in that daredevil.

"Mary Brown," I said to her with all of the gentleness in my voice that was commanded by my sympathy for her, "if a person were going to kill with a rope the man I loved I would lay down my own life that he should live. If you write one little paper to say that he murdered in defense of you, the good Gouverneur Faulkner will save him to you. Give to me that paper."

"Go away," she moaned as she shook her head and cried into her arms.

"See, Mary: Here is the pencil and the paper to write the words of life for Timms to that Gouverneur Faulkner," I said as I seated myself beside her and extracted my notebook and pencil from the pocket of my overcoat where I had placed them on leaving my room as is always best, I deemed, for a secretary. "There are just two things that are the duty of women, Mary: to bear men and to save them. Save yours now, Mary. Much will happen, it may be; but that Timms is a good man and must live."

"I dassent. He told me not to, Timms did."

"If a knife was aimed at Timms' heart, would you not throw yourself between him and its cut, Mary, even though commanded by him not to so save him?"

"Yes!"

"The knife is aimed and here's the paper by which you can throw your person on that knife. Is it of such moment that it cut into your own heart, that you stand and let it give death to him?"

"I give up! I give up, Mister! I can't let nobody murder him. Nobody ever put it that way to me. Give me that paper and let me git to him fer jest one minute to-morrow," she made answer to me as she seized the paper and pencil and began to write with the paper spread beside her upon the step.

"I will myself send you in my car with good black Kizzie to see Timms to-morrow, Mary," I promised her while she wrote.

"I got ter get my arms around his neck once more 'fore he kills me fer telling," she answered as she signed her name to the paper and handed it to me.

"Place those arms in that position, Mary, before telling him of your action and all will be well," I advised of her with much wisdom.

"Will that do, Mister?" she asked with anxiety as I began to fold the paper.

On that paper she had written:

"Hen Timms had locked me in the room and was forcing me when Gabe broke in and got me away from him. He had to bust his head with a flatiron to make him let go of me. I am a good woman.

Mary Brown"

"Yes, good Mary, this will shield Timms from that knife, I feel a certainty, and I will send for you and see that you go to an interview with him at ten o'clock of the to-morrow morning. And now good night, with great respect to you for a brave woman," I said as I rose to my feet.

"Who are you, Mister, that have spoke to my heart like they ain't nobody spoke to its suffering yet, though you ain't said many words and them is curious like?" she asked of me as I prepared to take a hurried departure.

"I am the secretary of the Gouverneur Faulkner, Mary, and - and - I know - how women - love - men. I -"

"I bet a many of 'em have loved you, God bless your sweet eyes. Good night, sir!"

And with those kind words from the poor female, who was beginning again to sob but with another motive in her weeping, I took my departure down the street - or up - I did not know in just which direction. I had the intention of returning to the house of Madam Taylor to obtain the Cherry, which I had left standing before her door, and in it convey the message to my Gouverneur Faulkner that should bring relief to his anxiety, but I soon found that I had lost myself upon streets that I had never seen before.

What was it that I should do? My heart suffered that my Gouverneur Faulkner should not know the relief of that paper I had in the pocket of my dinner coat, but I could not find myself and I did not know exactly what questions I should ask. Then I bethought me of that telephone, which in America is so much used, but not in France. I entered into a store for medicines upon the corner of one of the streets in my wandering, looked diligently in a book to find the number for the Mansion of the Gouverneur, and after many tellings of my desire, at last my Gouverneur Faulkner made an answer in my ear that was as beautiful in voice as the words he spoke to me in his presence.

"Well?" he asked of me.

"This is Robert Carruthers who speaks."

"Oh, all right, youngster. How did the fatted pie go?"

"That was a very nice pie, Your Excellency, and I have a paper from that Mary Brown concerning the murder of the brother of good Timms for cruelty to Mary. I wish to give it to you."

"What do you mean, boy?"

"I have said it."

"Then bring it here to me at once and tell me how you got it."

"I cannot come to you."

"Then I'll come to you. Where are you?"

"I do not know. I am lost."

"God, boy, what do you mean?"

"I am in a store of medicine that is many streets from that house of good Mary Brown, and also from the house of Madam Taylor. I have the intention of calling on the telephone my faithful Bonbon and asking that he come and find me and deliver me to the home of Madam Taylor and from thence transport this paper to you that you go to sleep for a much needed rest."

"You helpless young idiot, call a taxi and come right here to me."

"I am promised to a dance with Mademoiselle Belle by the hour of ten, of which it lacks now only a quarter. Cannot I go in that taxicab, which it is of much intelligence of you to suggest to me, and send by that taxicab to you the paper from Mary Brown while I stay to dance that dance?"

"Well I'll be - no, I can't say it over the telephone."

"What is it, my Gouverneur Faulkner?"

"I'll say it in the morning to you in person. I'll just hold up the wheels of state until that dance is over. Go ahead, youngster; call the taxi and get back to Belle. I'll have Jenkins waiting at the Taylor's to get the paper and you can - can tell me all about it in the morning. Will nine o'clock be too early to call you from - your rosy dreams?"

"I do not have coffee until nine o'clock, my Gouverneur Faulkner, and I do not make a very hurried toilet, but I will come to you at the Capitol at that nine o'clock if you so command - very gladly."

"Oh, no, we'll all of us just - just cool our heels until you get your coffee and toilet. Don't hurry, I beg of you! Good night, and beat it to Belle, as Buzz would say. Good night, you - you - but I'll say it all in the morning if it takes a half day. Good night again." And with that parting salutation my Gouverneur Faulkner's voice died from the telephone with what I thought had the sound of a very nice laugh.

That Mademoiselle Belle Keith is a dancer of the greatest beauty, and also is the homely Mildred Summers. The two hours until midnight at the home of my lovely Madam Taylor seemed as one short half of an hour to me. I also had the pleasure of conducting the nice Belle home in the Cherry so that I could make a fine display to her of my skill with a motor. In France it would be of a great scandal to allow a beautiful *jeune fille*, as is that Belle, and a nice gentleman, such as I declare Mr. Robert Carruthers to be, to go out into the midnight alone and unattended; but is it that in America the gentlemen are of a greater virtue than in France, or is it that the ladies have that great virtue? I do not know, but I declare it to be of much interest to remark.

"You'll find old Forty-Two Centimeter firing off overtime, L'Aiglon, because when the Whitworth gang got caught up on those specifications they side-stepped with another proposition and he's scouting for holes in it. Better climb the grapevine into bed and side-step him," advised Buzz to me while we waited beside our cars for the beautiful Belle and beautiful Sue.

"Much gratitude for your advice, and good night," I called to him as we separated the Cherry and the Gray and went in diverse directions.

I understood that "climb the grapevine into bed" to mean entering my home and that of my Uncle, the General Robert, with much stealth and that thing I did, dropping into a deep sleep in the moment of inserting myself between the sheets of that bed.

And when I awakened, because of that much dancing, behold, it was ten of the clock and eleven thereto before I arrived in a very great hurry with much pinkness of cheeks in the office of the Gouverneur Faulkner at the Capitol of the State of Harpeth.

And in that office I also discovered my Uncle, the General Robert, performing the action of the forty-two centimeter gun with words about my extreme lateness.

"You young fox trotter, you, I'd break every bone in your body if I wasn't so damned proud of you," he exploded directly in front of me.

"General, if you'll let me take Robert into his office for five minutes alone I'll help you take the hide off of him later," said that Gouverneur Faulkner as he beamed the great kindness to me. "Just stay here and get that Timms pardon crowd ready to hear the news of Mary's confession and I'll tell you all about it when I've settled with Robert."

"Very well, sir, very well," answered my Uncle, the General Robert, with a further explosion of words. "I'll also expect you to give him commands about this dance the young females in this town are leading him." With which my Uncle, the General Robert, himself went into the anteroom and left me alone with the beloved Gouverneur Faulkner.

"Good morning, Robert," he said to me with a laugh as he came and stood close beside me. That Roberta, Marquise of Grez and Bye, will blush within me, when that beloved Gouverneur comes very close beside her, in a way that is an embarrassment to Robert Carruthers, his secretary. "And now tell me what you said to that stupid Mary Brown that made her see the light," he asked me with his fine eyes looking into mine with a great interest and something of admiration.

"I asked of her if she would not throw herself before that beloved good Timms if a knife was aimed at his heart; and she perceived from that question that she must give to me the paper. A heart that has felt a great tragedy draw near a beloved one can speak without words to another who sees also a beloved in danger. Is it that you slept in ease, my Gouverneur Faulkner, after you had received that paper? It grieved me that you should sit at work while I was at dancing," I answered to him as I drew nearer and laid my hand with timidity upon the sleeve of his coat.

"My God, boy, do they grow many like you in France?" was the answer that the great Gouverneur Faulkner made to me as he looked down into the adoration of my eyes raised to his, with a question that was of deep bewilderment.

"France has grown many young and fine men who - who die, my Gouverneur Faulkner for her in the trenches, where I must soon go," I answered him with my head drawn to its entire height in the likeness of the old Marquis of Grez and Flanders.

"When you go into the trenches of France, youngster, the State of Harpeth will have a Governor on leave in the same trench," answered me that Gouverneur Faulkner with a very gentle hand laid on the sleeve of my coat above the bandages of my wound, and a glow of the star in his eyes. "Brothers by bloodshed, Marquis of Grez and Bye."

"Roberta, Marquise of Grez and Bye, how will you even gain the refuge of your petticoats and get away from these lies of dishonor if you are to be so pursued by -" I was asking of myself when my Uncle, the General Robert, opened the door and said:

"Better see this pardon delegation now, Governor. That other matter is going to go to hell as fast as it can if we don't scotch it. Robert, get those letters on your desk into United States as quickly as possible. That French deluge is upon us. Come back as soon as you can." With which I was dismissed into my own small anteroom.

And what did I find in those letters?

CHAPTER XV

"BEHOLD, I AM A SPY!"

As I sat and held in my hand those papers in which were two long messages, the one written in a very poor English and the other in a very elegant French, the woman Roberta, Marquise of Grez and Bye, trembled with fear of a discovery of her woman's estate while that daredevil Robert Carruthers raged within and also turned with a deadly hatred and distrust of the greatest gentleman that *le bon Dieu* had ever given to him to know. It was as I say, and for this reason: In the letters were announcements of the arrival of the Lieutenant, Count Edouard de Bourdon, on that Tuesday which the Madam Whitworth had mentioned. They were written with great ceremony to my Uncle, the General Robert Carruthers, as Secretary of the State of Harpeth, to give to him that information to be conveyed to His Excellency, the Gouverneur Faulkner, in due form though he already had that information.

"They make into a fool my revered Uncle, the General Robert Carruthers, who would keep his State and the Gouverneur of that State from dishonor!" I exclaimed to myself in my rage. "And this woman thinks to play with the life of French soldiers as she has with that same Gouverneur Faulkner, does she? No, there is Roberta, Marquise of Grez and Bye, who is a soldier of her Republique by appointment from the great Capitaine, the Count de Lasselles, to both watch and further the interests of France, whom she must meet in combat first!"

And as I said these words to myself I made a rapid writing of both papers and with them asked admittance to the room of that false Gouverneur Faulkner, who had just dismissed the good men who had come to thank him for his mercy shown to that poor creature Timms.

"Walk right in, sir," said old Cato to me as he gave a low bow of very great courtesy. Then he looked with eyes of great keenness into my stormy face. "Make a cross on the floor with that hoodoo in your shoe, little mas', ef you git in danger or need of luck," he whispered to me, coming very close. And as he directed I so performed at the very entrance of the audience chamber of the great Gouverneur of the State of Harpeth. Then, with a fine relief on his face, good Cato flung open the door and announced me with great ceremony.

In that room I found my Uncle, the General Robert, and the Gouverneur Faulkner in deep consultation and they both turned towards me with anxiety in their faces.

"What did you make of the letters, boy?" asked my Uncle, the General Robert, with keen anxiety. The great Gouverneur was silent and for the first time since I had looked into his face my eyes did not glance in his direction.

"They both announce the arrival on Tuesday of the

Lieutenant, the Count de Bourdon, to sign the contracts concerning the mules to be sold by the State of Harpeth to the Republique of France, sir," I answered in a cold and formal voice and then stood at an attention for any more questions.

"The devil they do!" exclaimed my Uncle, the General Robert, while still the Gouverneur Faulkner was silent. "Do they give no excuse for being nearly ten days ahead of time, sir?"

"No, honored Uncle," I answered. "Madam Whitworth said to me that the Gouverneur Faulkner had set that date for the arrival of the Commission, and had so informed her; and I think that to be the reason for absence of such excuses." And as I made that answer, which was one of great impertinence from a secretary to a chief who was a great gouverneur, I looked with cold calmness into the dark star eyes under their black lashes, which were darting lightnings of anger at my words.

"God!" exclaimed my Uncle, the General Robert Carruthers, and he turned white with a trembling as he faced the lightning in those eyes of the stars. But it was not to his Secretary of State that the great Gouverneur Faulkner made his denial but to his humble secretary, Robert Carruthers, who looked without fear into the very depths of those lightnings.

"This is the first time I have heard of a change of date for the arrival of the commission, Robert," he said in a calm voice as for a second his eyes held mine, a second which was sufficient for a truth to pass from his heart and still the storm in mine. I did not understand all that his eyes said of a great hurt but I knew that what he spoke was true and would always be.

"And what were you doing gossiping with that lying hussy, sir?" demanded my Uncle, the General Robert, with instant belief in the word of that Gouverneur Faulkner, turning his anger upon me, who stood and took it with such a joy in my heart from the truth that had come into it from those eyes of the night stars, that I did not even feel its violence.

"*Vive la France* and the State of Harpeth! Behold, I am a spy!" I answered him as I drew myself to my greatest height and gave the salute which his old soldiers give to him at that raising of the banner of the Cause that he had lost in his youth.

"You young daredevil, you, I'm a great mind to break every bone in your body, as I have said before," he said to me, but I could see a smile of pride making a lightning of the gloom in his countenance over the trouble of his affairs of state. "You keep away from -"

"Robert," was the interruption made by my great beloved Gouverneur Faulkner, "upon you will fall the task of making the plans for the entertainment of this countryman of yours. The General and I will be too busy getting-ready-to-meet-them-on-their-own-grounds to give any time to that. Remember, they will have to be shown the best grazing land in the valley, in motor cars. When they are done sizing us up, we'll be ready for them. The Count and his secretaries will, of course, be entertained at the Mansion and you can make arrangements at the hotel for the rest of the suite. Also will you please instruct my servants, from Cato down, how to make them comfortable and, Robert, will you confer with Mrs. Whitworth, who, as the wife of the Treasurer of the State of Harpeth while neither the General nor I have wives, must be considered as the official social representative of the State, as to what form the official entertainments must take?" And as he asked that question of me my Gouverneur Faulkner did not so much as glance at my Uncle, the General Robert, who gave an exclamation of contempt in his throat as he began a reading of the two papers which I had handed to him.

"Also I suppose this means I must give up all hope of services from that fly-up-the-creek, Clendenning," he grumbled as he read.

"I will do as you bid me, my Gouverneur Faulkner, in all things, and I will be much helped by both my excellent Buzz and the beautiful Madam Whitworth," I made answer to the question and command given to me by the Gouverneur Faulkner, and as I mentioned the name of that lady I lowered my eyes to the floor and waited for my dismissal. I did not want to look into his eyes, for I did not know even then if I might not find that Madam Whitworth there. I only knew that whatever she did or was to him, his honor was inviolable.

"Well, get to it all," commanded my Uncle, the General Robert. "Get vouchers for what you spend and pay with State Department checks. Don't blow in a fortune, you young spendthrift, you, but also remember that the State of Harpeth is one of the richest in America and knows how to show France real hospitality."

"That State of Harpeth has shown that hospitality to one humble youth of France, my Uncle Robert, who has a great gratitude," I made answer to him as I laid my cheek upon the sleeve of his coat, which was of a cut in the best style for gentlemen of his age but always of that Confederate gray, likewise affected by good Cato. Try as hard as Robert Carruthers will, he cannot force that Roberta, Marquise of Grez and Bye, at all times to refrain from a caress to the Uncle whom she so greatly loves.

"Clear out, sir! Depart!" was the response I got to that caress; but always that wicked Roberta, Marquise of Grez and Bye, finds in the face of her relative something that assures her that she can so venture at a later time.

And as I turned away from that coldness on the part of my august relative I found a glow of warmth for my reviving in the eyes of my beautiful Gouverneur Faulkner, who held out his hand to me as I started to the door for that departure commanded me.

"Blood brothers never doubt each other, Robert," he said to me as with one hand he grasped my right hand and laid the other on my above my bandage, over the wound Timms had given to me, which was now almost entirely healed.

With the quickness of lightning I laid my cheek against the sleeve of his coat, in exactly the caress I had given to my Uncle, the General Robert, and then did depart with an equal rapidity.

"Can you beat him, Bill?" I heard my Uncle, the General Robert, demand as I closed the door.

"Impossible," was the answer I thought was returned.

And from that audience chamber I went quickly and alone in my good Cherry to Twin Oaks, was admitted by Bonbon, whom I instructed not in any way to allow that I be interrupted, ascended to my own apartment and seated myself in a large chair before the glowing ashes of a small fire of fragrant chip twigs, which kind Madam Kizzie had had lighted, against what she called a "May chill," during my toilet of the morning. Above me from the mantelshelf, that Grandmamma Carruthers looked down with her great and noble smile, while the flame in her eyes seemed to answer that in my soul as I communed with myself.

"What is it that you will now do, Roberta, Marquise of Grez and Bye?" I asked of myself with a slight shaking of my knees in their cheviot trousers. "It is hardly possible that you will escape from revealing your woman's estate to this Frenchman of your own class. Here all mistakes of a man's estate are forgiven you and laid to the fact of your being an alien, but that Lieutenant, Count de Bourdon, will ask questions of you and perhaps has a knowledge of your relatives and friends - indeed, must have. Also, already that wicked Madam Whitworth entertains suspicions of you. What is it that you will do?"

And after I had asked myself for a second time that question I sat and looked into the eyes of that Grandmamma Carruthers for many long moments and had an argument with myself; then I answered to her as I rose to my feet so that my eyes came more nearly on a level with hers:

"No, Madam Ancestress, born of her whom not an Indian or a fierce bear could frighten away from her duty of protection to those of her affections, I will not flee. I will stay here by the side of my Uncle, the General Robert, and my great chief, that Gouverneur Faulkner, to fight for their honor and to protect France from robbery. Then, if I be discovered and can do no more for them, I will go from their presence quickly in the night and be lost in the trenches of France before I am detained. And if it be that I am not discovered before all is made well concerning those mules for transportation of food to the soldiers of France, then I will still go away to the battlefields of France before it is discovered by all who have given affection to Robert Carruthers, that he is a - lie. I will leave love for me and for France in all of these kind hearts, which will comfort me when I fight for the Republique, or live for her during long years. I grieve exceedingly; but I go!"

And after that long conference with myself I called upon the telephone my Buzz and asked of him that he meet me at the Club of Old Hickory, of which, after the required time of waiting, I was soon to be an enrolled member.

And when I told to my Mr. Bumble Bee the fact that in the space of barely three days the great gentleman of France would be in Hayesville for the purpose of a visit and the signing of the contracts concerning our much discussed friend, the mule, he gave a very long and loud whistle and placed his elbows upon the smoking table between us.

"Well, this does call for hustle," he said as he knocked from his cigarette the ashes. "What are your plans, L'Aiglon?"

"I do not know what it is best to plan, my Buzz," I answered in perplexity. "Of course, there must be the official reception by His Excellency, the Gouverneur Faulkner, upon the evening of their arrival, but more I cannot think. Also, I am commanded by His Excellency to consult the beautiful Madam Whitworth as the only official wife of the State, on account of the title of Treasurer of her husband."

"Oh, Mrs. Pat will be satisfied to shine at the elbow of Governor Bill at the reception and we can trust her to arrange little odd cosy hours for herself and any of the bunch who pleases her. It's the man end of it we want to handle."

"Yes, it is that man end you speak of I wish you to perform for me, my Buzz," I assented eagerly.

"I'll tell you what let's do," exclaimed that Buzz with a very great light of enthusiasm coming into his countenance. "Let's don't try to imitate London, Paris or New York in blowing 'em off; let's give them a taste of the genuine rural thing. Let's take the bunch down to the Brice stock farm, Glencove, give 'em a barbecue done by old Cato and let 'em see the horses run. Gee, they have got a string of youngsters there! It will take two and a half days, for it's fifty miles down over a mighty poor road, but it's worth it when you get there. The Brice farm is the heart of the Harpeth Valley. We took that English Lordkin, who came to visit Governor Bill last year, down to see old Brice, and it took us ten days to get him to break away."

"That we will do, my fine Mr. Bumble Bee," I answered with gratitude.

"Sure, it's the thing," said my Buzz with conviction. "We pass right through the grazing land of the State and we can show them the mule in the making - the right kind of mule. We'd have to do that anyway, for that is what they are here for."

I feel a certainty that if I should continue to be an American man for all of the days I may live, to that three score and ten age, I would never be able to gain in any way even a small portion of what my fine Mr. Buzz Clendenning calls "hustle." I went at his side for the three days which intervened between the news of the arrival of that Lieutenant, Count de Bourdon, and that actual arrival, in what seemed to me to be the pace of a very fleet horse or even as the flight of a bird. And as fast as we went from the arrangement of one detail of entertainment to another, the beautiful Madam Whitworth went with us, with her eyes of the flower blue very bright with a great excitement. I was glad that in all matters it was necessary that my fine Buzz also consult with her and thus I was not exposed to any of her wickedness alone.

And in my own heart was also a great excitement, for it seemed to me that I was fighting a great battle for France all alone. All day I could see that that Mr. Jefferson Whitworth and the other men of wealth who with him were seeking to be robbers to my Country, were first in consultation with themselves and then with my Uncle, the General Robert, and also the Gouverneur Faulkner. Would their powerful wickedness prevail and be able to force a signing of that paper on the Gouverneur? Was that in their power, I asked of myself, and in my ignorance I did not know an answer and had no person to demand one from. There was no ease of heart to me, when the days went by and I was so at work with my Buzz that I had no time for words from my Gouverneur Faulkner or glance from those eyes of the dawn star. I could only murmur to myself:

"*Vive la France* and Harpeth America!"

CHAPTER XVI

"IMMEDIATELY I COME TO YOU!"

And so the time passed until the morning upon which the same railroad train which had brought young Robert Carruthers down into the valley home of his forefathers, arrived with yet another son of France and his secretaries and servants. All were in attendance at the station of arrival, from the Secretary of State, the General Carruthers, who in his large car was to take the Count de Bourdon to the Gouverneur's Mansion for immediate introduction, down to good Cato in a very new gray coat and a quite shiny black hat.

"Stand right alongside, Robert," commanded my Uncle, the General Robert, as he arranged with impatience a large white rose I had placed upon the lapel of his very elegant gray coat. "I never did like heathens. They make my flesh crawl. Be sure and repeat slowly all he says, damn him!"

"He will speak to you in English very like unto that I use, I feel sure, my Uncle Robert," I said with a great soothing.

"He will not, sir, he will not!" answered my Uncle, the General Robert, with a great impatience. "Half the blood in your veins is the good red blood I gave you, sir, and never forget that. Look what a man it has made of you!"

"Yes, my Uncle Robert," I answered with a great sadness but also some amusement. In my heart I prayed that always when I had left him he would think that blood to be the good red blood of a man of honor and not of a woman of lies. It might be that some day he would be proud that still another man of his house had died in battle for France and - never know.

It was while my eyes were covered with a mist of tears that I heard the great railway train approaching, which was perhaps to bring me my dishonor, and I drew those tears back into my heart and stepped forward to the steps of the car from which I could see a very slight and short but very distinguished looking Frenchman about to descend.

"I thank the good God I have never before encountered him," I said in my heart as I stood in front of him.

"Lieutenant, the Count de Bourdon, I make you welcome to the State of Harpeth, in the name of my Uncle, the Secretary of that State," I said to him in the language of his own country as I clapped together my heels and gave to him the bow from the waist of a French gentleman who is not a soldier. "Will you permit that I lead you to that Uncle?"

"Many thanks, Monsieur, is it Carruthers I name you after your distinguished relative?" he made answer to me as he returned my bow with first one of its kind and then a military salute.

" Robert Carruthers , sir, and at your service," I made

answer to him with a great formality. And as I spoke I saw that he gave to me a glance of great curiosity and would have asked a question but at that moment my Uncle, the General Robert, stood beside us.

"I present to you the General Carruthers, Secretary of the State of Harpeth, Monsieur the Lieutenant, the Count de Bourdon of the forty-fourth Chasseurs of the Republique of France." I said with again a great ceremony and a very deep bow.

"I'm mighty glad to welcome you to Old Harpeth, Count. How did you make the trip down? said my Uncle, the General Robert, as he held out his large and beautiful old hand and gave to the Count Edouard de Bourdon such a clasp that must have been to him most painful. And as I beheld that very tall grand old soldier of that Lost Cause look down upon that very polished and small representative of the French army, that American eagle began a flapping of his wings against the strings of my heart where I had not before discovered him to reside.

"But he is not as my Capitaine, the Count de Lasselles," I said in reproof to that eagle, which made a quiet in my heart so that I could listen to the words returned by the man of France to the man of America.

"I thank you, Monsieur the Secretary of Harpeth; my journey was of great pleasure and comfort," were the words which he returned in very nice English.

"Then we'll go right up and see Governor Faulkner at the Capitol before lunch, Count, if that suits you," my Uncle, the General Robert, said with a very evident relief at those words of English coming from that

French mouth. "Here's my car over this way and this is Mr. Clendenning, who'll look after the rest of the gentlemen in your party and bring them on up to the Capitol."

"Monsieur," said the Lieutenant, Count de Bourdon, with another bow and then a quick recovery as he saw that he must take the hand of Buzz, held out to him in great cordiality. These handshakes of America are very confusing to those of Europe.

I saw a great laughter almost to explosion in the eyes of my Buzz at the very little man who had such a great manner, and I made a hurrying of him and my Uncle, the General Robert, to the large car standing beside the station.

"I will precede you in my Cherry," I said as I saw both the gentlemen seated together upon the back seat of the large black machine.

"No you don't; you take your seat right in here with us, to be on hand if any bridge of this international conversation breaks down under the Count and me," answered my Uncle, the General Robert, with stern command.

"Is it that the young Monsieur Carruthers had an education in France?" asked the Lieutenant, the Count de Bourdon. "He has the air of French - shall I say, youth?" And as he spoke again I saw a gleam of deeply aroused interest in his eyes which made my knees to tremble in their tweed trousers.

"Born there; son of my brother, who died at the Marne," made answer to the question my Uncle, the

General Robert.

"It is now that I make a remembrance. That Capitaine Carruthers was the husband to the very beautiful Marquise de Grez and Bye. In her youth I was her friend. I did not know - " but as the Lieutenant, the Count de Bourdon, was making this discovery which sent a thrill of fear into the toes of my very shoes, the car stopped at the main entrance of the Capitol and halfway down the long flight of steps stood His Excellency, the great Gouverneur Faulkner of the State of Harpeth, waiting to receive the guest who came on a mission to him from a great land across the waters. Until I die and even into a space beyond that, I shall take that picture of magnificence which was made by my beloved Gouverneur Faulkner as he stood in the May sunlight with his bronze hair in a gleaming. I thought him to be a great statue of Succor as he held out both of his strong hands to the smaller man who had come from a stricken land for his help.

"*Le bon Dieu* keep of his heart a friend of France," I prayed as I watched those hands clasp as my Uncle, the General Robert, made the introduction.

And all the long hours of that long day were as dreams of sadness and fear to me as I went about the many duties of entertainment laid upon me. At luncheon at that Club of Old Hickory I sat opposite the small Frenchman who sat on the right hand of my Gouverneur Faulkner, and opposite to me sat my Uncle, the General Robert. No business was in discussion at that time but I could see those eyes of French shrewdness make a darting from one face to another and ever they came back to me with a great puzzle which gave to me terrible fear.

To all the plans for his entertainment he gave an assent of delight and for that two days' journey down into the grazing lands of the Harpeth Valley he had a great eagerness until told that it was to be undertaken upon the morrow.

"Is it not that we will be occupied on the morning of to-morrow with the signing of those papers of importance, Your Excellency?" he asked with a grave annoyance which was under a fine control.

"The Secretary of State, General Carruthers, and I think it will be best that you see the grazing lands of Harpeth and some of the mules being put into condition before the signing of the contracts," was what was "handed out to him," as my Buzz would have expressed it, by my Gouverneur Faulkner with a great courtesy and kindliness as he helped himself to some excellent chicken prepared in a fry. I could see a great start of alarm come into the eyes of that small Lieutenant, the Count de Bourdon, at those calm words, but he gave not a sign of it. In my heart was a great hope that something had been discovered for the protection of my soldiers of France, and I also took to myself a portion of that excellent chicken and did make the attempt to consume it as I beheld all of those great gentlemen performing. I believe that under excitement men possess a much greater calmness of appetite than do women.

"Monsieur le Gouverneur, it is not necessary that I behold those lands and those mules; the signature of the great Gouverneur of the State of Harpeth will make a mule to grow from a desert, in the eyes of the French Government," he said with a smile of great charm spreading over his very small countenance.

Maria Thompson Daviess

But just at this moment, when a reply would have been of an awkwardness to make, the music, which is made by a most delightful band of black men for all eating in that Club of Old Hickory, began to play the great Marseillaise, and with one motion all of the gentlemen in that dining room rose to their feet in respect to the distinguished guest of that Old Hickory Club. Also many friendly glances were cast upon me, which I returned with a smile of great gratitude.

"Yes, the pen is mightier than the mule stick in his eyes, the scoundrel," remarked my Uncle, the General Robert, as I drove to the Capitol with him in his car, while the Gouverneur Faulkner took his guest with him in his.

"Is any proof been found that he shall not do this robbery to France, my Uncle Robert?" I asked with great eagerness.

"Trap is about ready to spring, but not quite. God, but Jeff Whitworth is a skilled thief! I know what he is up to but I can't quite get it on the surface. Keep the French robber busy, boy, for a little longer, and I'll land him. Here we are at the office! Now you get busy keeping them busy - and I'll land 'em. If not, I'll go and show France what real fighting is and I'll take you with me into the worst trench they've got! Battles, indeed - they ought to have been at Chickamauga. Now depart!" With which words my Uncle, the General Robert, got out of the car and left me to direct it to wherever I chose.

"I have a warmth at heart that the three men most beloved of me would go onto the French battle line with me," I murmured to myself as the black chauffeur drove me back to that Club of Old Hickory to get me again in company of my Buzz. "And yet it is the custom of women to believe that they command the deepest affection of which a man is possessed. And, *helas*, it is believed to be impossible for a comrade that he be also a lover!"

It has been my good fortune to be one of the guests at many very brilliant receptions of much state in some of the very grand and ancient palaces of the different countries of Europe, but at none of them have I seen a greater brilliancy than at the one given in his Mansion by the Gouverneur Faulkner of the State of Harpeth in America. All of that old Mansion, which has the high ceilings and the decorations of a palace, if not quite the size, was adorned with very large masses of a most lovely and handsome flower, which is of many shades of a pink hue set in dark and shining leaves and which is called the rhododendron. There were many lights and music of a softness I have never heard equaled, because the souls of those black men seem to be formed for a very strange kind of music. Also I had never beheld women of a more loveliness than those of the State of Harpeth, who had come from many small cities near to Hayesville at an invitation of very careful selection for their beauty by my Buzz.

"Let's give him a genuine dazzle," he had remarked while making a list for the sending of the cards.

And most beautiful of all those beautiful *grande dames* was that Madam Patricia Whitworth, who, with her husband, stood at the side of His Excellency, the great Gouverneur Faulkner, for the receiving of his guests. Her eyes of the blue flowers set in the snow of crystals were in a gleaming and the costume that she wore was but a few wisps of gossamer used for the revealing of her radiant body. In my black and stiff attire of the raven I stood near to the other hand of the Gouverneur Faulkner and there was such an anger for her in my heart that it was difficult that I made a return of the smile she cast upon me at every few minutes. Was there a mockery in that smile, that she had discovered my woman's estate and was using her own beauty for a challenge to me? I could not tell nor could I judge exactly what the smile of boldness which the Lieutenant, the Count de Bourdon, cast upon me, might mean. And in doubt and anxiety I stood there in that great salon for many hours to make conversation with the guest of honor easy with those who came to him for presentation, until at last I was so weary that I could not make even a good night to my Uncle, the General Robert, when we entered, long after midnight, the doors of Twin Oaks.

When in my own apartment, alone with the beautiful Grandmamma, I cast myself upon the bed upon which my father had had birth, and wept with all my woman's heart which beat so hard under that attire of the raven.

"Scarcely one more day and perhaps I must flee in dishonor from all the love of these friends," I sobbed to myself, but deeper than all that I wept for the picture of that beautiful woman at the side of my beloved Gouverneur Faulkner.

And then suddenly as I lay in my weeping the telephone upon the table beside my bed gave a loud ringing in the darkness that was long after midnight. Very quickly from fear I covered my head with my pillow and waited with a great fluttering of heart.

Then a second time it rang with a great fury and I perceived that I must make a response to it.

I arose and took that receiver into my hand and spoke with a fine though husky calmness.

"What is it?" I asked.

"Is that you, Robert?" came the voice of my beloved Gouverneur, which made the heart of that anguished Roberta, Marquise of Grez and Bye, beat into a sudden great happiness though also alarm.

"Yes, Your Excellency."

"Can you dress very quietly, get your car and come up here to the Mansion without letting anybody know of it?"

"I will do what you command."

"I need you, boy, and I need you quick."

"I come."

"Stop the car at the street beyond the side door and come in that way. Cato will let you in. Come to my bedroom quietly so as not to wake Jenkins. Can you find your way?"

For just one single long second that *grande dame*, Roberta, the Marquise of Grez and Bye, cowered in fear upon her warm bed in the house of her Uncle, the General Robert, at the thought of going out into the night at the command of a man, and then that devoted daredevil, Mr. Robert Carruthers, answered into the telephone to the Gouverneur Faulkner:

"Immediately I come to you."

CHAPTER XVII

THE TALL TIMBERS OF OLD HARPETH

Is it that there comes to the world an hour in the twenty and four in which it lays aside the mortality of the earth and clothes itself in an immortality of a very great awe? I think that it is so; and it was out into the whiteness of that hour that I stepped when I had successfully passed from my room to the garden of the home of my Uncle, the General Robert, which is also the home of my American ancestors. A command for my presence had come to me from the loved Gouverneur Faulkner and it was needful that I make all possible haste; but it seemed to me that all of the beautiful faded flowers of my dead grandmammas in that garden rose up around me for beguilement and gave to me a perfume that they had kept in saving for the Roberta, some day to come across the waters to them. And all of their little descendants, the opening blossoms of spring, also gave perfume to me in a mist in the white moonlight, while a few fragrant rose vines bent to detain me as I left that home of my grand-mothers to go out into that sleeping city, alone. I had a great fear, but yet a great devotion drew me and in a very few minutes I had driven my Cherry from the garage and was on my way through the silent streets to - I did not know what.

Maria Thompson Daviess

At the door of the Mansion I was admitted by my good Cato, who was attired in a very long red flannel sleeping garment, with a red cap also of the flannel tied down upon the white wool of his head.

"Has you got dat hoodoo, little Mas'?" he demanded of me as I passed into the hall beneath the candle in a tall stand of silver which he held high over my head.

"Yes, good Cato," I made answer to him and I was indeed glad that I had now of a habit put his gift under the heel of my left foot. It gave me great courage.

"De Governor is up in his room and you kin go right up. I never heard of no such doings as is going on in dis house dis night with that there wild man with a gun five feet long, coming and going like de wind. Go on up, honey, and see what you kin do to dem with dat hoodoo." With which information good Cato started me up the stairs. "First door to the right, front, and don't knock," he called in a whisper that might have come from his tomb in death as he slowly retired into the darkness below with his candle.

For a very long minute I stood before that door in the dim light that came through one of the wide windows from the moon without.

"What is this madness that you perform, Roberta, Marquise of Grez and Bye?" I made demand of myself while my knees trembled in the trousers of heavy gray worsted.

"Robert Carruthers goes to his chief in an hour of need and he is descended of that Madam Donaldson who had no fear of the Indian or the bear when there was danger to her beloved," I made answer to myself and softly I turned the handle of that door and entered the room of the Gouverneur Faulkner.

"Is that you, Robert?" came a question in his voice from a large table over by the window. The room was entirely in shadow, except for the shaded light upon the table, under whose rays I remarked the head and shoulders of that Gouverneur Faulkner, at whose bidding I had come out into the dead of the night. "Come over here and walk softly, so as not to stir up Jenkins," he commanded me and I went immediately to his side, even if I did experience a difficulty in the breath of Roberta, Marquise of Grez and Bye.

"What is it that you wish, my Gouverneur Faulkner?" I asked as I looked down upon him as he sat with a paper in his hand regarding it intently. And as I looked I observed that he, as well as I, had not entirely disrobed after that very brilliant reception. He had discarded his coat of the raven and also what is called a vest in America, and he was very beautiful to me in the whiteness of his very fine linen above which his dark bronze hair with its silver crests, that I had always observed to be in a very sleek order, was tossed into a mop that resembled the usual appearance of my own. His eyes were very deep under their heavy lashes but of the brilliancy of the stars in the blackness of a dark night.

"Sit down here under the light beside me," was his next command to me, and he reached out one of his slender and powerful hands and drew me down into a chair very close beside him.

" What is it?" I asked as my head came so close to his

that I felt the warmth of his breath on my cold cheek.

"Hold these two fragments of paper together and translate the French written upon them literally," he said to me as he handed me two small pieces of paper upon which there was writing.

And this is what I discovered to be written:

"Honored Madam:

"The one at the head of all has sent me to this place to inspect grazing lands and make report. I send in a report of what is not here and the signing of the papers by your Gouverneur Faulkner must be done quickly in blindness before a discovery of what is not -"

"It is written to a woman," I said very quietly as I made a finish of reading.

"Yes, boy, to a woman. I have made my last fight to - to hold an old belief, which in some way seemed to be - be one of my foundation stones. The General is right: they are all alike, the soft, beautiful, lying things. The truth is not in them, and their own or a man's honor is a plaything. That piece of paper was sent me by a man up in the mountains of Old Harpeth, who loves me with the same blood bond that I love you, boy, all on account of a gun struck up in the hands of his enemy. Here's the note he sent with it.

"Bill, we cotched a furren man fer a revenue up by the still at Turkey Gulch and this was in his pocket. I made out to read yo name. I send it. The man is kept tied. What is mules worth? Send price and what to do with this man critter by son Jim. Hell, Bill, they ain't no grazing fer five thousand mules on Paradise Ridge, but I know a place.

Jim Todd."

"What is the significance of this paper, my Gouverneur Faulkner?" I asked after I had made the attempt to translate to myself the very peculiar writing he had given to me.

"I do not know just exactly myself, Robert," answered my Gouverneur Faulkner as he dropped his head upon his hands while he rested his elbows on the polished table among its scattered papers. "I am convinced now that this mule contract business is the plot against my honor that the General believes it to be and has been trying to get to a legal surface. In some way Jim Todd has got hold of one end of the conspiracy. It has been hard for me to believe that a woman would sell me out. If I take it to her in the morning I'll perhaps get an explanation that will satisfy me. The men who are in with Jeff Whitworth are the best financiers in the State and it is impossible to believe that -"

Very suddenly it happened in my heart to know what to compel that very large man beside me to do for the rescue of his honor. He must see the matter, not through the lies of that beautiful Madam Whitworth, the instrument of that very ugly husband, but he must look into the matter with his blood friend, that Mr. Jim Todd.

"You must go immediately to that Mr. Jim Todd and his prisoner to discover truth, Your Excellency," I said with a very firm determination as I looked straight into his sad eyes that had in them almost the look of shame for dishonor.

"It's twenty-four hours on horseback across Old Harpeth from Springtown, boy. The trip would take three days. I can't do it with these guests here, even if they are robbers. I'll have to stay and dig down to the root of the matter here. I may find it in the hearts of my friends," he answered me with a look of great despair.

"The root of the matter is that man who is a prisoner, my Gouverneur Faulkner. I say that you go; that you start while yet it is night and while no man can advise you not to take that journey. It can be done while this entertainment to the farm of the Brices is made for the inspection of mules and also the running of horses. It is necessary!" As I spoke to him in that manner a great force rose in me that I poured out to him through my eyes.

"Great Heavens, boy, I believe I'll do it. I could never get anything if I went when they knew I was going, but I might find out the whole thing if I went to it in secret. If I go now they'll not have time to get their breath before I am back. I'll be able to think out there is those hills and I'm - a - man who needs to think - with a vision unobscured." For a long minute my Gouverneur Faulkner sat with his head bowed in his hands as he rested his elbows on that table, then he rose to his feet. "Let's get away while it is still the dead of night, Robert. I'll leave a note with Cato to tell the General that I've taken you, and nobody except himself must know where I have gone or why. He'll put up the right bluff and we'll be back before they get anything out of him. It's three o'clock and we must be far out on the road by daybreak. We'll take your car and leave it in hiding at Springtown, where by sunup we'll get horses to cross the mountains."

"Is it that I must go for three days out into those mountains with you, my Gouverneur Faulkner?" faltered that ridiculous and troublesome Roberta, Marquise of Grez and Bye.

"Why, no, Robert, unless - unless - Oh, well, I suppose this prisoner of Jim's can speak English as they all can. I rather wanted you - but perhaps it is best for me to fight it out alone. Will you help me pack a bag? Get the one from my dressing room while I take a plunge."

"Quick, Robert Carruthers, make an excuse to that Roberta, Marquise of Grez and Bye, who is of such a foolishness, that you must go with your beloved Gouverneur Faulkner for his aid," I said to myself.

"It is necessary that your foreign secretary accompany you to deal with that gentleman of France who is in prison, my Gouverneur Faulkner," I said with decision as I rose from the side of the table with a great quickness. "I must return home for a few necessities of my toilet for those three days, but I will be back in what that good Kizzie says to be a jiffy, when speaking of cooking that is delayed."

"Good," answered me my beloved Gouverneur Faulkner. Then he laid his hand upon my shoulder as we stood together in the dimness out from the rays of the light. "There is something in your eyes, Robert, that renews my faith in the truths of - of life. I'm going out into the wilderness on a grave mission whose result may shake down some houses of - of cards, but because of your being with me I feel as if I were starting off on a picnic or a day's fishing at the age of ten. Now, I'll hurry." And as he spoke my Gouverneur Faulkner made a start in the direction of his room for the bath.

"Is it that I may begin the packing of your bag for you, Your Excellency, before I go for those necessities of my own?" I asked of him.

"Won't be time for you to go home, boy," he answered me, looking at a clock upon the mantel over his large fireplace. "You are still in your evening clothes, I see. But that's easy: you climb into that pink coat and a pair of those corduroy trousers of mine you see hanging in my dressing room. I haven't hunted for two years but they are still there. Put linen in that saddlebag on the shelf for us both out of the drawers in the old chest over there. Take heavy socks to go under the leggings. You'd better put on a flannel shirt, too, and take an extra one for both of us. We'll travel light. I'll only be in the bath a couple of minutes." With which assurance he entered the room of the bath and closed the door upon me.

"*Mon Dieu*, Roberta, Marquise of Grez and Bye!" was all that I allowed myself to exclaim as I made a very quick rush for that dressing room, switched on the light, flung off my coat, seized a pair of corduroy riding breeches that hung in a corner beside another pair, discarded my own of broadcloth and struggled with both of my legs the same moment into them. Then in a hurry as great as I shall ever know I discovered a gray flannel shirt in a drawer of the very tall old mahogany chest and inserted myself into that with an equal rapidity. A wide leather belt made the two very large garments secure around my waist and I again allowed breath to come into my lungs. I then opened a very queer bag which I knew to be for a saddle, that was upon a shelf in the dressing room, and began to put things into it according to directions of the Gouverneur Faulkner. The other pair of those riding breeches I laid with another of the flannel shirts in a great conspicuousness upon a chair in the bedroom directly in front of the door from the dressing room.

"We're going to make a record get-away, boy," said that Gouverneur Faulkner to me as in a few minutes he came, clothed in those riding trousers and that flannel shirt, to the door of his dressing room, where I was just making a finish of putting needful clothing into his bag. "You'll find the other things we need in the bathroom. Put it all in while I get together a few papers I want. We can start now in two minutes."

"All is ready now, my Gouverneur Faulkner," I made the announcement after a wading into that very wet room of the bath and a return.

"Here, give me the bag, and you go ahead with this electric torch. Quiet now," admonished that Gouverneur Faulkner to me as we took our departure through the dark hall.

"This is the maddest escapade that a Governor of this ancient State has ever undertaken, and the weight of years has slid from me, boy," said that Gouverneur Faulkner to me as the Cherry made a long glide from the city out into the open road.

The day was just beginning to come with its light from behind the very large and crooked old mountain that is called Old Harpeth, when my Gouverneur Faulkner made me to turn my good Cherry from off the main road into a little road, of much narrowness and of beautiful brown dirt the color of the riding trousers that I wore, and stop beside a very humble, small house, which was covered with a vine in beautiful bud, and around which many chickens hovered in waiting for a morning breakfast. Behind the small house was a large barn and as I made a nice turn and stop beside the white gate a man in a blue garment that I now know is called overalls, came to the door of the barn.

"Hello, Bud. Are Lightfoot and Steady in good condition for a trip across to Turkey-Gulch?" called my Gouverneur Faulkner as he alighted from the car.

"Fit as fiddles, Governor Bill," answered the man as he came to the gate to shake hands with the Gouverneur Faulkner. "'Light and come in to breakfast. Granny has got a couple of chickens already in the skillet. And say, I want you to see what Mandy have got in the bed with her. Ten pounds, Gov."

"Congratulations, Bud; that is some - boy?" said my Gouverneur Faulkner with a question as he again grasped the hand of the large man.

"Naw, Gov; we didn't have no luck this first shot but I tells Mandy that we've got about a dozen more chanstes if she does as well by me as she oughter. Anyway what's the matter with a gal child?" And the nice young father of the poor little female made a bristle of his disposition in defense of his daughter.

"Not a thing on earth, Bud; except that the whole sex are the unknown quantity. This is my secretary, Robert Carruthers, the General's nephew. Come in, Robert, and you'll have one square meal in your life if you never get another. Get me the usual food wallet together, Bud, please, and let me have it and the horses the very moment I've swallowed the last bite of my drum bone, will you? We've got to ride fast and far to-day and I want nobody on my trail. Understand?"

"Yep, Gov," was the answer that good Bud man made as my Gouverneur Faulkner and I took our way through many chickens into the low little house.

"God bless my soul, if here ain't the Governor come for a bite with Granny Bell this fine morning!" exclaimed a very nice old lady from above a stove, which was steaming with food of such an odor as to create a madness in my very empty stomach.

"More than any bite, Granny," answered my Gouverneur Faulkner as he came beside the stove to shake hands with the nice hostess.

"I'd like to feed you some gold, fried in silk. Governor Bill, fer that mercy to my nephew Timms. I can't say what I feels and finish this cream gravy the right color for you," and as she spoke the fine old friend of my Gouverneur Faulkner wept as she shook a steaming sauce in a black pan and turned with the left hand a golden piece of bread upon another part of the stove.

"I don't need anything more than your 'well done,' Granny," answered my Gouverneur Faulkner as he laid a gentle hand on the trembling shoulder of the nice old lady. "This youngster here got the word from Mary and you can give him both of the liver wings if you want to show your gratitude to him."

"God bless you, young gentleman, and you shall have

anything that Granny Bell has to give you in gratitude. Now draw up two chairs and fall to, boys," and as she spoke she set the dishes of a beautiful odor upon a very clean table beside the stove.

"Is it that I may wash the grease stains of the car from my hands before eating, dear Madam?" I asked of her.

"Back porch, you'll find the bucket and pan and towel, youngster. I can't wait for you," made answer my Gouverneur Faulkner as he laughed and began upon the repast that must of necessity be a hurried one.

CHAPTER XVIII

THE CAMP HEAVEN

And I was very glad indeed that he did not go with me for that toilet to my hands, for it might have happened that a noise would have deprived me of a very beautiful thing that I discovered, through a window under a vine of roses that opened upon that back porch.

A very pretty young girl, with hair the color of the maize in the fields, lay upon a white bed beneath a quilt of many colors. Her sleeping garment was drawn back from her breast, against which lay a little human person drinking therefrom with much energy. The eyes of the mother were closed and her arm held the babe loosely as if in a deep dreaming. I softly poured the water into the basin, made clean my hands and quietly withdrew into the kitchen, with much care that I did not awaken her. On my cheeks I could feel a deep glow of color, and something within my heart pounded with force against my own breast under its gay red coat of a hunting man. I could not raise my eyes to those of my Gouverneur Faulkner and I ate not as much of that good breakfast as Robert Carruthers could have consumed if the woman in his heart had not been so stirred.

And all of that long day in the soft early spring which

Maria Thompson Daviess

was bursting into a budding and a flowering under the feet of our horses and above our heads in the trees, it was the woman Roberta that rode at the side of my Gouverneur Faulkner, with her heart at an ache under her coat of a man. It was with a difficulty that I forced my eyes to meet and make answer to the merriment and joy of the woods in his deep ones; and I was of a great gladness when the descending of the sun brought a moon-silvered twilight down upon us from the young green branches of the large trees of the forest through which we rode.

"Time to make camp. We've got to old Jutting Rock. You are halfway up between heaven and earth, youngster," said my Gouverneur Faulkner as he drew to a halt his horse in front of me and pointed down into the dim valley that lay at our feet.

"I am glad that we have made this Camp Heaven," I answered to him as I slid from my horse, ungirthed him, and drew from his back the heavy saddle he had worn for the day, as I had been taught by my father to do after a day's hunting, if no grooms came immediately. "Is it that you have hunger, my Gouverneur Faulkner?"

"Only about ten pounds of food craving," he made answer to me with a large laugh that was the first I had ever heard him to give forth. "I'll rustle the fire and water if you'll open the food wallet and feed the horses."

"Immediately I will do all of that," I made an answer to him and because of the happiness of that laugh he had given forth, a gladness rose in my heart that made me again that merry boy Robert.

And it was with a great industry for a short hour that we prepared the Camp Heaven for a sojourn of a night. Upon a very nice hot fire I put good bacon to cook and my Gouverneur set also the pot of coffee upon the coals. Then, while I made crisp with the heat the brown corn pones, with which that Granny Bell had provided us, he brought a large armful of a very fragrant kind of tree and threw it not far into the shadow of the great tree which was the roof to our Camp Heaven.

"Bed," he said as he came and stood beside the fire in a large towering over me. I dropped beyond rescue a fragment of that corn bread into the extreme heat of the coals, but I said with a great composure and a briefness like unto his words:

"Supper."

"Why is it that a man thinks he wants more of life's goods than fatigue, supper and bed, do you suppose, boy?" questioned my Gouverneur Faulkner to me as at last in repletion he leaned back against our giant rooftree, between two of whose hospitable large roots we had made our repast, and lighted a pipe of great fragrance which he had taken from his pocket.

"I would not possess happiness even though I had this nice supper, if I was alone in this great forest, Your Excellency; I would have fear," I answered him with a small laugh as I took my corduroy knees into my embrace and looked off into that distant valley below us which was beginning to glow with stars of home lights.

"Didn't I tell you once that you don't count, that you

are just myself, youngster? You ought not to know I am here. I don't know you exist except as a form of pleasure of which I do not ask the reason," was the answer that my Gouverneur Faulkner made to me.

"I excuse myself away with humbleness for impertinence, Your Excellency," I returned to him.

"If you tried, do you think you could call me Bill, just for to-night, boy?" was the answer he made to my excuses as he puffed a beautiful ring of smoke at me.

"I could not," I answered with an indignation.

"I heard you call Sue Tomlinson 'Sue' the first night you danced with her."

"But that Mademoiselle Sue is a woman, my Gouverneur Faulkner," I answered with haste.

"That's the reason that women get at us to do us, youngster; we don't approach them as human to human but we go up on their blind side and they come back at us in the dark with a knife." And as he spoke all of the gayness of joy was lost from the voice of my beloved Gouverneur and in its place was a bitterness.

"With pardon I say that it is not a truth of all women, Your Excellency," I answered with pride as my head went up high at his condemnation of the sex of which I was one.

"You don't know what you are talking about, youngster. They all think I am cold and pass me along, except a few experienced ladies who - shall I say? - adventure for graft with me. I've been too busy really to love or let love but I know 'em and you don't. Let's stop talking about what concerns neither of us and go to bed. See this young cedar tree? I'm going to throw my blanket across it and with these extra boughs I'll make a genuine cradle for each of us on the opposite sides of the trunk. Then we'll cover with your blanket and be as comfortable as two middies in their hammocks in a man of war. This is a piece of woodcraft of my own invention and I'm proud of it, old scout."

And while he talked my Gouverneur Faulkner had prepared those cradles of our blankets unstrapped from the saddles of the horses at feeding time, seated himself upon the edge of one of them and began to pull from his feet his riding boots. "Take off your boots and your coat, youngster, and turn in. I'll take the wind-ward side and you can bivouac against the fire. Good night!" As he finished speaking my Gouverneur Faulkner rolled beneath that blanket upon the outer edge and left for me the hammock next to the fire, sheltered from a cool wind that had begun to come up from the valley.

Almost immediately, so that I should not have a fright, I lifted the blanket and crawled into the branches of the fragrant tree. Even as I did so I perceived a loud breathing of deep sleep from my Gouverneur Faulkner; but to me came no repose.

Awake through the bright night, I lay there in the sweet branches of the young tree beside the great Gouverneur of one of the greatest states of America and perceived clearly the pass to which my course of lies and dishonor had led me. And from that wild daredevil, Roberta, Marquise of Grez and Bye, was born the honest woman Roberta who must extricate herself from a situation not to be longer endured, even if discovery was not upon me.

"I will finish this journey with my beloved Gouverneur Faulkner," I counseled myself, "upon which it is of a certainty that this plot for his ruin in the world of his politics will be averted, and I will return to the home of my Uncle, the General Robert. If I be not discovered in my woman's estate in a few days' space of time I will endeavor to do some piece of loving kindness that will keep me in the memory of all who have given me love, from poor black Bonbon up to His Excellency himself here beside me, and then I will go into those trenches of France to give my life for my country, perhaps not as a soldier but as a good nurse of the Red Cross. And never, never, must any living person who has loved Robert Carruthers know that he is a human of dishonor. Nannette will be true to my directions to hide my secret, and wee Pierre will keep it forever because I go to fight for France as he cannot. I will put with great firmness into the mind of Pierre that he is to be of a great devotion to my Uncle, the General Robert, through life.

"And what will you do for that great Gouverneur Faulkner, from whom each day you have stolen more and more affection with your false attitude of much loyalty, to keep from him grief at the loss of you?" I asked myself with a sob in my heart.

"Forgive me, my beloved chief. When away from you I must die of a coldness," I said to myself in a very low tone into the moonlight.

"Cold ? Do you want the whole blanket, youngster?

Snuggle into your cradle closer," suddenly answered me my Gouverneur Faulkner as he reached his long arm across the tree trunk to tuck in the blanket about me and again he was immediately in the deep sleep from which my spoken words had but partly awakened him. And then at his bidding I did settle myself down into the fragrant boughs and I wept myself also into a deep sleep.

The round sun was high over that Old Harpeth hill when I opened my eyes. For a moment I did not see clearly and then I looked straight into the deep eyes of my Gouverneur Faulkner. which for that first time I had been able to see to be the color of violets in the twilight. He was seated beside me smoking the fragrant pipe and looking down at me with a great wonderment that was mingled with as great a tenderness.

"Boy," he asked softly, "are you sure God has got that pattern of you put away carefully in France?"

Before I could make answer to him a picture flashed into my mind. When still a child one morning I opened my eyes to find my loved father bending over me and in the hollow of his arm he held my mother in her breakfast gown of lace and ribbons. He spoke:

"Some day, Celeste, a man will bend over her and watch her waken. God grant it will be with the love - that produced that beauty. Look at that love curl!"

And at the recall of that picture of me into my mind, my hands flew to my face to find that same treacherous curl had descended to my cheek from the mop above. With a fury of embarrassment I sprang to my feet from under that blanket.

Maria Thompson Daviess

"I have a great hunger," I said as I observed a very crisp breakfast to be prepared upon the coals of the fire. "I must have a fragment of bacon upon the instant." And I bent over the fire to obtain what I had demanded for a cover to my confusion.

"No, you don't, until you've washed that face and those hands that still have the supper smudge on them, in the pool down there. I left the soap and the dry sleeves and bosom of a flannel shirt for you. Don't you pack towels in a kit in your country?" With which laughing answer my Gouverneur Faulkner denied unto me an immediate breakfast.

"You thought him to admire the love curl, while he was remarking the soil upon your face, Roberta, Marquise of Grez and Bye," I laughed to myself as I plunged my face into the icy pool.

After a finish to the breakfast, my Gouverneur Faulkner gave to me the information that we must tether the good horses and make the remainder of the journey by walking, which we did for hardly a short hour.

"The wildcat still is straight up Turkey Gulch and we'll have to scramble for it. It's hid like the nest of an old turkey hen," he said to me as we set out upon the mounting of a very steep precipice.

"What is that word, 'wildcat still'?" I asked as I slid over a great rock with emerald moss encrusted, and struggled beside my Gouverneur Faulkner through a heavy underbrush of leafy greenness.

"A place where men make whiskey in defiance of the

law of their State," he answered me as he held aside a long branch of green that was pink tipped, so that I might slip thereunder without a scratching.

"Are you not the law of the State, my Gouverneur Faulkner?" I asked of him as I pulled myself by his arm through the thickness.

"I'm all that, but I'm the son of Old Harpeth and Jim Todd's blood brother first. Some day I'll smoke Jim out of his hole and get him a good job. Now, wait a minute and see what happens," and as he spoke my Gouverneur Faulkner stood very still for a long minute. As I sat at his side upon the fallen trunk of a large tree I regarded him with admiration, because he had the aspect of some beautiful, lithe animal of the woods as he listened with a deep attention. Then very quickly he put his two long fingers to his mouth, and behold the call of a wild bird came from between his lips. Twice it was repeated and then he stood again in deep attention. I made not even a little breathing as I too listened.

Then came three clear notes of that same wild bird in reply from not very far up the mountain from us.

"That's Jim, the old turkey; come on!" said my Gouverneur Faulkner as he again began to break through the leafy barriers of the low trees.

And in a very short space of time a man emerged from a little path that led behind a tall cliff of the gray rocks. He was a very large and a very fierce man and I might have had a fright of him if his blue eyes had not held such a kindness and joy in them at the sight of my Gouverneur Faulkner.

"Howdy, Bill," he said with no handshake or other form of a comrade's greeting.

"Howdy, Jim," returned my Gouverneur Faulkner in a manner of the same indifference but with also an expression in his face of delight at the sight of his blood brother, that Mr. Jim Todd.

"That thar boy a shet-mouth?"

"He's Bob, and as hard as a nut," was the introduction I had from my Gouverneur Faulkner.

"Then come on," with which command that wild man led us around the tall cliff of gray rock, over which climbed a sweet vine of rosy blossoming, which I now know to call a laurel, and we arrived in front of a small and low hut that was built against the rocks. A clear, small stream made a very noisy way past the door of the hut, but save for its clamor all was silent.

"Where are the boys?" asked my Gouverneur Faulkner.

"Hid in the bushes. I've got the man tied back in the still room. I 'low he ain't no revenue but they 'low different. Come back and see if you kin make out his gibberish."

"Come on, Robert," said my Gouverneur Faulkner to me as he followed the wild Jim into the hut and back into a room that was as a cave cut into the rock. And I, Robert Carruthers, followed him - to my death.

Seated upon a rude bench in that cave room, bound with a rope of great size, disheveled and soiled, but with all of the nobility of his great estate in his grave face, was my adored friend, Capitaine, the Count de Lasselles! As we entered he rose beside the bench and in that rising displayed a chain by which one of his feet was made fast to the rock of the wall.

"Good morning, sir," said my Gouverneur Faulkner, as if greeting a gentleman upon the street of that city of Hayesville.

"Also a good morning, sir," made reply my poor Capitaine, the Count de Lasselles. And he stood with a fine and great courtesy waiting for my Gouverneur Faulkner to state to him what his visit could portend, as would he have done in his regimental room at Tour.

And as he stood, for that very long minute, there expired the last moments of the life of Robert Carruthers. A stream of light fell from the little window high in the rock upon his luckless head as he stood as if frozen into a statue of great fear. And as he so stood, the eyes of the Capitaine, the Count de Lasselles, fell upon him and he started forward as far as the length of the chain by which he was bound would allow him and from there held out his hand to the frozen boy standing in the stream of light from high heaven.

"My most beautiful lady Roberta, do I find that it is you who have come to my rescue?" he questioned. "I lost you, *mon enfant*, in that great New York."

"My beloved Capitaine, how is it that I find you thus?" I exclaimed as I went to within his reach and allowed that he take my two hands in his poor shackled ones and put warm kisses of greeting upon them.

And it was while I was shedding tears of pity for the imprisonment of that great man of France in that mountain hut in America, as he kissed my hands, that I raised my eyes to encounter a cold lightning as of a flash on steel, from under the black brows of my Gouverneur Faulkner of the State of Harpeth, that again froze the blood in my heart.

"You?" he asked of me in a voice that was of the same coldness and sharpness as that steel, and his beautiful mouth was set into one straight line as he flung into my face that one word.

CHAPTER XIX

ALL IS LOST

And to that word of challenge I made no answer, but I raised my head and looked into his eyes with a dignity that came to me as my right from suffering. So regarding each other, we stood for a very short minute in which the Capitaine, the Count de Lasselles, raised his head from his kisses of salutation upon my hands.

"And, *mon enfant*, is this the good Uncle to whose care you came into America?" asked that Capitaine, the Count de Lasselles, as he reached out his imprisoned hands for a greeting to my relative.

I did not make any answer to that question. My head raised itself yet higher, and I looked my Gouverneur Faulkner again full in the face while I waited to hear what he would answer of my kinship to him.

"Sir, I am the friend of General Carruthers and I am also the Governor of the State of Harpeth. I have come across the mountains to talk with you about the business of this contract for mules for your army and I have brought your young friend to assist me if I should need translating from or to you. We Americans, Captain, are poor handlers of any language not our own, and the matter is of much gravity." And as the

Gouverneur Faulkner spoke those words to my Capitaine, the Count de Lasselles, with a great courtesy but also a great sternness, in which he named me not as his friend but as the friend of that Capitaine, the Count de Lasselles, I knew that I was placed by him among all women liars of the world and that to him his boy Robert of honor was of a truth dead forever.

"It is indeed of such a gravity that I have come from the English Canada to make all clear to myself," answered my beloved Capitaine, the Count de Lasselles, as he drew himself to his entire height, which was well-nigh as great as that of the Gouverneur of the State of Harpeth.

"And I have ridden a day and a night, sir, for the same purpose," answered my great Gouverneur Faulkner with that beautiful courtesy of business I have always observed him to use in the transaction of his affairs in his office at the Capitol of the State of Harpeth. "And as one of us must make a beginning, will you not tell me, Captain, why you are here and in this predicament?"

"In a few words I will make all clear to you, Your Excellency," made answer my Capitaine, the Count de Lasselles, with an air of courtesy equal to that of the Gouverneur Faulkner. "I sent down into your State of Harpeth one of my Commission, to whom I gave the direction that with a lack of annoying publicity he should investigate the preparedness of the State of Harpeth to deliver those five thousand of mules to the Republique of France as was being proposed. Behold, a report that all is well comes to me, but - ah, it is with sorrow and shame that such a thing could be done by a son of poor France who struggles for life! - among the sheets of that report was left by mistake the fragments of a draft of a letter to an American woman, which made a partial disclosure of an intended falseness of that statement to me. Immediately I came alone to interview that false officer and I find him gone from that small town not far from here into your Capital. I was seeking to rapidly ride alone by directions into your Capital city to prevent that he make a signature, which I had given to him the authority to write, to those papers of so great an importance. I was thus arrested by that man of great wildness, whose *patois* I could not understand as he could not comprehend the English I make use of, and you see me thus. I beg of you to tell me if that wicked signature has been made."

"The papers have not been signed, thank God, Captain, and your very impatient lieutenant is being shown some Southern hospitality by the flower and chivalry of Old Harpeth. And I beg your pardon for allowing you to be a prisoner a minute longer than necessary," was the answer made to him by my Gouverneur Faulkner. "Untie the Captain, Jim; he's all right. And you can bring us a little of your mountain dew while I clear this table here to use for the papers of our business." And still my Gouverneur Faulkner did not speak or look at me and in my heart I then knew that he never would.

"I will make all ready," I said as I lifted a large gun, a horn of a beast full of powder and several pipes with tobacco, from the table of rough boards that stood under the window for light.

"Ah, that is a good release! Thank you that you did not make tight enough for abrasions your cords, my good man," said my Capitaine, the Count de Lasselles, as he stretched out his arms and then bent to make a rubbing of his ankle upon which had been the chain.

"I said you warn't no revenue. Here, drink, stranger!" answered the wild Jim as he handed a bottle of white liquid to my Capitaine, the Count de Lasselles, and also another to my Gouverneur Faulkner. "That boy can suck the drippings," he added as he looked at me with humor.

"Get cups and water, Jim," commanded my Gouverneur Faulkner with a smile. "Don't drink it straight, Captain. It will knock you down."

"I will procure the cups and the water," I said with rapidity, for I longed to leave that room for a few moments in which to shake from my eyes some of the tears that were making a mist before them.

"Git a fresh bucket from the spring up the gulch, Bob, while I go beat the boys outen the bushes with the news that they ain't no revenue. They'll want to see Bill," was the direction that wild Jim gave to me as he placed in my hand a rude bucket and pointed up the side of the hill of great steepness. After so doing he descended around the rock by the path which we had ascended.

"What is it that you shall do now, Roberta, Marquise of Grez and Bye?" I wept a question to myself as I dipped that bucket into a clear pool and made ready to return to the hut. "All is lost to you.

"I do not know," I answered to myself.

And when I had made a safe return to the hut with a small portion of the water only remaining in the bucket, for the cause of many slides in the steep descent from the pool, I found my Gouverneur Faulkner and my Capitaine, the Count de Lasselles, engaged deeply in a mass of papers on the table between them and with no thanks to Roberta, the Marquise of Grez and Bye, when she served to them tin cups of the water and a liquid that I had ascertained by tasting to be of fire. I believe it to be thus that in affairs of business, in the minds of men all women are become drowned.

"Will you write this out for His Excellency, my dear Mademoiselle?" would request my good Capitaine, the Count de Lasselles.

"Thank you," would be the reply I received from the Gouverneur Faulkner of the State of Harpeth, with never one small look into my eyes that so besought his.

And for all of the hours of that very long afternoon I sat on a low stool beside the feet of those two great gentlemen and served them in their communications while the heart in my breast was going into death by a slow, cruel torture.

The exact meaning of those papers and words of business I did not know, but once I observed my Capitaine, the Count de Lasselles, throw down his pencil and look into the face of the Gouverneur Faulkner with a great and stern astonishment.

"The work of grafters, Captain Lasselles, with a woman as a tool. But I yet don't see just how it was that she worked it. My Secretary of State, General

Carruthers, and I have been at work for weeks and we could not catch the exact fraud," made answer my Gouverneur Faulkner with a cold sternness.

"I was warned in Paris that beautiful American women were very much interested in the placing of war contracts, Monsieur le Gouverneur. I fled upon a tug boat from the ship that I escape some for whom I had letters of introduction which I could not ignore."

"It was your Capitaine, the Count de Lasselles, whom that Madam Whitworth sought upon the ship, Roberta," I said to myself.

"I think women are alike the world over, Captain, and the discussion of them and their mental and moral processes is - fruitless," answered my Gouverneur Faulkner as he again took up his pencil.

"When it happened to me to find the fragment of the letter to the lady of America from my false lieutenant, I had a deep distress that tenderness for the sufferings of poor France should fail to be in even one American woman's heart. And now I am in deep concern. Where am I to obtain the good strong mules by which to transport through fields heavy with mud the food to my poor boys in their trenches?"

"Right here, Captain, I feel reasonably sure. I think I see a way to give you what you want at a better figure; and from it no man shall reap more than a just wage for honest work. As the Governor of the State of Harpeth, I can give you at least that assurance." And as he spoke my Gouverneur Faulkner looked the Capitaine, the Count de Lasselles, in the eyes with a fine honesty that carried with it the utmost of conviction.

"I give thanks to *le bon Dieu*," I said with words that were very soft in my throat, but at which I observed the mouth of that Gouverneur Faulkner to again become as one straight line of coldness.

"Indeed, thanks to *le bon Dieu*, Mademoiselle," made courteous answer to me my Capitaine, the Count de Lasselles. "But how will you accomplish that purpose. Monsieur le Gouverneur?"

"As soon as I've done with these figures I'll have in Jim, your jailer, and then you'll hear some things about the American mountain mule that you never heard before, I believe." As he spoke, my Gouverneur Faulkner proceeded with making figures with his pencil, a fine glow of eagerness added to that of rage in his eyes very deep under their brows. "Now, I'll go and call in Jim," he said after a few minutes of waiting, and left the room in which I was then alone with my Capitaine, the Count de Lasselles, who came to me with outstretched hands.

"Ah, Mademoiselle Roberta," he exclaimed, "I am in a debt of gratitude to you for bringing this great gentleman, your friend, to my rescue and also to the solving of this very strange situation concerning these contracts. Indeed have you accomplished the mission for which you enlisted: your 'Friends for France.' But before procedure I must ask you, little lady, why it was that you made a vanishment from that hotel of Ritz-Carlton in New York. I sought you. I sought out that Monsieur Peter Scudder to inquire for you. Behold, he also is in sorrow over the loss of you and had for me a strange news of a cup of tea thrown in the face of that

Mr. Raines of Saint Louis by a member of your family who had departed immediately into the south of America. I said to myself, 'The beautiful child does not know that your heart is in anxiety for her,' and immediately I intended to seek you in the city, to which the very fine lady, who had reported that 'tea fight' as she so spoke of it to her paper, directed me after my finding of her. It is a great ease to my unhappy heart to find you in the care of a family and friends. I make compliments on your costume of the ride. I also observed the custom of attire masculine to be on those plains of the great West where I sought the wheat."

"It is a great joy to me, *mon Capitaine*, that you give to me your approval. Much has happened to me in these short weeks since you left me in loneliness on that great ship that I must tell to you," I said as a sob rose into my words.

"Poor little girl, it will not be many hours now before I can say to you the things that have been growing in my heart for you since that night upon the ship," he said to me in a great tenderness as he raised my hand and bent to kiss it just as entered the great Gouverneur Faulkner and the wild Jim.

I had not the courage to gaze upon the face of my Gouverneur Faulkner, but I felt its coldness strike into my body and turn it to hardness.

For a second I stood as a stone, then a sudden resolve rose in me and again that daredevil seized upon my thought. I took a piece of that white paper with caution and also a pencil, and with them slipped from the room, while that wild Jim seated himself upon my lowly stool beside the table at which again the two great men were writing.

And out in the soft light that was now slowly fading from the side of the mountain because of the retirement of the sun, I sat me down upon the step of the hut and wrote to my Gouverneur Faulkner this small letter:

"Honored Excellency, the Gouverneur Faulkner, of the State of Harpeth:

"I go from you into the trenches of France. If your humble boy Robert has done for you any small service, I beg of you in that name that my Uncle, the General Robert, and my friends never know of my dishonor of lies about my woman's estate, but believe me to die as a soldier for France as will be the case. Make all clear for me to my Capitaine, the Count de Lasselles. It is that all women are not lies.

Roberta, Marquise of Grez and Bye."

Then I left that letter upon the doorstep, held in place by the weight of a stone, and very softly slipped out into the shadows of the twilight and down the mountain by the path up which that morning I had come with my beloved Gouverneur Faulkner, then my friend. I felt a certainty that as many as two hours would those men continue in a consulting with that wild Jim and in that time by going fleetingly I could gain the place where were tethered the horses, before a complete darkness had come. From my honored father I had learned the ways of woods in hunting and also I knew that the good Lightfoot would in darkness carry me in safety to his stall in the barn of Mr. Bud Bell, beside which stood my Cherry. From there I could gain the city of Hayesville in the dead hours of the night and in those same dead hours depart to France, after obtaining the money I had left in my desk and which I had earned by my labors and would not be in the act of stealing from the State of Harpeth. Only one night and day would I be alone in the forest and I did not care if a death should overtake me. In my body my heart was dead and why should I desire the life of that body?

And as I had planned I then accomplished. I discovered that Lightfoot at pasture and I quickly had placed the saddle upon him and had turned him down the mountain to choose a safe path for both himself and me. I did not look upon those cradles of fragrant boughs in which the boy Robert had lain at rest beside his great friend, the Gouverneur Faulkner, from whom he had stolen faith and affection.

"Why did not you also steal his pocketbook as he lay asleep beside you, Roberta, Marquise of Grez and Bye?" I questioned myself with scorn and torture, as good Lightfoot crashed down from that Camp Heaven into the dark night.

And on we rode, the large horse with the woman upon his back, for a long night, through fragrant thickets that caught at my riding breeches with rose tendril fingers and under thick forests of budding trees, through whose branches of tender leaves the wise old stars looked down upon my bitter weeping with nothing of comfort, perhaps because they had grown of a hardness of heart from having seen so many tears of women drop in the silence of a lonely night.

Then came a dawn and a noon and a twilight through which I pushed forward the large horse with great cruelty, only pausing beside streams to allow that he drink of the water and also to throw myself down on my face and lap the cool refreshment like do all humble things. And, when at last the stars were again there to look down upon me, we arrived behind the barn of that Bud Bell to find all in the little house at rest. I thought of that small child in sleep in the arms of that woman, and a great sobbing came from my heart as I threw myself into my Cherry, after giving a supper to good Lightfoot, and fled down the long road to the distant city of Hayesville that lay away in the valley like a great nest of glowworms in a glade of the leaves of darkness. And among those glowworms I knew that more than a hundred friends to me were beginning to go into sleep with deep affection in their hearts for that Robert Carruthers whom wicked Roberta, Marquise of Grez and Bye, was about to steal from them. I wept as I turned my Cherry through the back street and into the garage of my Uncle, the General Robert. Then I paused. All was quiet in the house and no light burned in the apartments of my beloved protector and relative. From the watch at my wrist I ascertained the hour to be half after ten o'clock, and I knew that he was safely in cards at that Club of Old Hickory, whose lists now bore the added one of another Robert Carruthers, man of honor and descendant of its founders. Also there was no light in the rear of the house in the apartment of that kind Kizzie, in whose affections I had made a large place. A dim light burned in the hall and I knew that there I would find my faithful chocolate Bonbon sitting upon a chair by the great door in a deep sleep. And in a very few minutes I so found him.

"It is hello there, good Bonbon," I greeted him.

"Howdy, Mr. Robert," he answered me by a very large

smile with very white teeth set in his face of extreme blackness. "The Gen'l said to call him on the 'fome as soon as you come."

"That I will attend to from my apartment," I answered him and then ascended the wide dark stairway with feet which were as a weight to my ankles.

Very slowly I entered that apartment and turned on the bright light. All was in readiness for me, and on the small table under the glass case that contained that beflowered robe of state of the dead Grandmamma Carruthers stood a vase of very fresh and innocent young roses.

"I would that I could remain and fulfill the destiny of a woman of your house, Madam Grandmamma," I whispered to her lovely and smiling portrait on the wall opposite. "I am the last of the ladies Carruthers but I have made a forfeit of that destiny and I must go out in the night again in man's attire to a death that will tear asunder the tender flesh that you have borne. Good-bye!"

Then I made a commencement of a very rapid packing, in one of those bags which I had purchased from the kind gentleman in the City of New York, of what raiment I knew would be suitable for a man in very hurried traveling. I put into it the two suits of clothing for wear in the daytime, but I discarded all of my clothing for the pursuits of pleasure. The bag was at that moment full and I did not know that it could be closed. Then I bethought me of that brown coat that had upon it the blood which I had been allowed to shed for my beloved Gouverneur Faulkner who was now lost to me.

"That I will take and discard the night raiment, to sleep 'as is' in the manner spoken of by my friend, that Mr. G. Slade of Detroit," I counseled myself as I laid aside the silken garments that I did so like and placed in their stead the bloody coat of many wrinkles.

After all of that was accomplished I went into a hot bath and again quickly began to assume my man's clothing, while from my eyes dripped the slow tears that bleed from the heart of a woman.

"You must make a great hurry, thief Roberta, for it draws near midnight and that is the hour that the train departs to the North," I cautioned my weeping self. "At that hour you go forth into the world alone."

And then what ensued?

Very suddenly I heard the noise of a car being drawn to the curb in front of the house and the rapid steps of a man progress along the pavings of brick to the front door, at which he made a loud ringing. In not a moment was the good Bonbon at my door with a knocking.

"The Governor is here to see you, Mr. Robert," he informed me.

"What shall you do, Roberta, Marquise of Grez and Bye?" I asked of myself. "How is it that you can be able to support the cold reproaches he will give to you while requiring that you stay to bring dishonor to your Uncle, the General Robert? You are caught in a trap as is an animal."

And then as I cowered there in my agony, very

suddenly that terrible daredevil rose within me and gave to me a very strange counsel. As it was speaking to me my gaze was fixed upon the robe of state of the beautiful Grandmamma.

"Very well, then, that great Gouverneur Faulkner can give his chastisement and lay his commands upon the beautiful and wicked Roberta, Marquise of Grez and Bye, in proper person, and not have the privilege of again addressing his faithful and devoted comrade Robert, who is dead. I, the Marquise Roberta of Grez and Bye, will accord to him an interview and in the language of this United States it will be 'some' interview!" With which resolve I turned to make an answer to the faithful Bonbon at the door.

"Where awaits His Excellency, the Gouverneur Faulkner?" I questioned to him.

"In the hall at the bottom of the steps," he made reply to me.

"Attend him into the large drawing room for a waiting and make all of the lights to burn. Say to him that I will descend in a very small space of time," I commanded.

"Yes, sir," he made reply and departed.

CHAPTER XX

"YOU ARE - MYSELF!"

And then in my wickedness I began to commit a desecration on the memory of my beautiful and honored Grandmamma Carruthers. I walked to that glass case in which reposed that gown of the beautiful flowered silk and took it therefrom and laid it upon a chair above the soiled riding breeches of corduroy I had so lately discarded. I opened the carved wooden box on the table underneath and took from it the silver slippers and the stockings of silk, also the lace fan and the silver band for the hair. Thereupon I walked to my mirror and commenced to make a toilet of great care but of a great rapidity.

My first action was to take down that lovelock and with the oil of roses to lay it in its accustomed place upon my cheek, which burned with a beautiful rose of shame and at the same moment with some other emotion that I did not understand; which emotion also made my eyes as bright as the night stars out in that Camp Heaven. The silver band held closely the rest of my mop and gave it the appearance of the very close coiffure which is the fashion of this day, and one very sweet young rose I put into it just above the curl with an effect of great and wicked beauty.

Maria Thompson Daviess

The coiffure having been accomplished, the rest of the toilet, from the slippers of the cloth of silver to the edge of fine old lace, now the color of rich cream, that rested upon the arch of my bare white breast was only a matter of a few moments, and then I stood away from my mirror and beheld myself therein.

"You are as beautiful as you are wicked, Roberta, Marquise of Grez and Bye, but you go to your death in a manner befitting a *grande dame* of your ancient house of France, whose daughters once showed the rabble how to approach a guillotine, costumed in magnificence. Descend for that cold knife to your heart!" And so speaking, I picked up my fan and made my way through the hall to the halfway of the wide steps. At that point a commotion occurred.

"Lordee! It's the old lady come to ha'nt!" exclaimed my good Bonbon and with a groan he fled into the darkness in the back regions of the house.

And it happened that his loud cry brought a response which came to me before I was quite in readiness for it. As I reached the last step of the wide staircase, under the bright light I raised my eyes, and behold, the Gouverneur Faulkner to whom I had descended for the purpose of mortal combat, stood before me!

And was it that cruel and wicked and cold Gouverneur Faulkner who was to scourge me and keep me in the house of my Uncle, the General Robert, for a dishonor? It was not. Before me stood a tall man who was of a great paleness and a terrible fatigue also, covered with the dust of a long, hard ride, with eyes that were full of a fear, who stood and looked at me with not one word of any kind.

Suddenly I bowed my head and stretched out my bare arms, the one of which bore the red scar from the wound suffered for him, and thus suppliant I waited to receive the reproaches that were due to me.

And for a long minute I waited and then again for another long period of time and no word came to me. Then I raised my head!

For all women now in the world who have the love of a man in their hearts, and for those unborn who will come into that possession, I pray that they may be given the opportunity to plant in the hearts of those men of their desire the seed of a fine loyalty and service and comradeship, and that they may some day look into his eyes and see that seed slowly expand into a great white flower of mate love, as I beheld bloom for me in the eyes of my beloved Gouverneur Faulkner. Long we stood there and looked into the soul of each other and let the flower grow, drinking from our hearts and the veins of our bodies until at last it was fully open; and then I went with a love cry into his arms held out to me, and pressed the heart of my soft woman's body close against his own.

"I think my heart has always known, though my mind's eyes were blind. God, if I had lost you into that hell of war, you daredevil!" he whispered and I tasted the salt of his tears on my lips.

"I am a lie," I whispered back to him.

"You are - myself," he laughed through a sob, and then, while with his large warm hand he held my throat as a person does the stem of a flower, he pressed his lips into mine until they reached to the heart within me.

In a moment with my hands I held him back from me.

"I must go, my beloved, even as I have said," I cried to him. "I cannot stay to my dishonor and to the rage and unhappiness my Uncle, the General Robert, will experience when he discovers that a girl has cheated him in his great affection and generosity to her.

"It *is* going to be hard on the General to have his grandmother come to life on his hands like this," laughed my Gouverneur Faulkner, bending and placing upon the creamy lace of my Grandmamma a kiss which was warm to my heart through the beflowered silk.

"Let me die in those trenches so that he will never know," I pleaded.

"No, sweetheart, that would be too easy. You are going to stay right here and face the old Forty-Two Centimeter," he made a reply to my pleading request as he bent and laid his cheek upon the lovelock. "That curl ought to have opened my eyes when I sat and watched you open yours day before yesterday morning," was the remark he added to his cruel command that I stay and face my very dreadful and so very much beloved Uncle, the General Robert.

"I am afraid," I answered as I clung to him with a trembling.

"Yes, I know you are afraid of him - or anything," laughed my beloved Gouverneur Faulkner with a shake of my bare shoulders under his strong hands. "But perhaps these papers I have in my pocket from Captain Lasselles, who is at the Mansion getting rid of dust, will help you out after the first explosion, which you will have to stand in a very few minutes from now, if that hall clock is correct and I know the General's habits as I think I do."

"Oh, let me ascend and get once again into my trousers!" I exclaimed as I sought to leave the arms that again held me close.

"Never," said my Gouverneur Faulkner after another kiss upon the lace on my breast. "You'll just wear this ball gown until you can get some dimity, Madam, and don't you ever even mention to me - "

But just here an interruption arrived, and I sprang from the arms of my Gouverneur Faulkner only in time to avoid being discovered therein. My beloved Uncle, the General Robert, entered the door in a great hurry, with that much frightened Bonbon following close at his heels.

"What's all this that fool nigger phoned about ghosts walking and - " Then he stood very still in the spot upon which his feet were placed and regarded me as I turned from the arms of my Gouverneur Faulkner and faced him.

"My God, Governor, what has happened to my boy?" he asked, and his fine old face was of a great whiteness and trembling. "Sam says he's dead and the ghost -" and then came another pause in which all of the persons present held for a long minute their breath.

Did I make excuses and explanations and pleadings to my beloved Uncle, the General Robert, in such suffering over the death of that Robert? I did not. I opened my strong young arms wide and took him into them with a tenderness of such great force that it would of a necessity go into his very heart.

"I am a wicked girl who has come to you in lies as a boy, my Uncle Robert, but I have a love that is so great for you that I will be in death if you do not accept of it from me," I said as I pressed my cheek in its tears against his.

And for still another long minute all of the persons present waited again and I forced to remain in my throat a sob, while my beloved Gouverneur Faulkner laid one of his hands on the shoulder of my Uncle, the General Robert.

And then did come that explosion!

"You young limb of Satan, you! I could shake the life out of you if I didn't prefer a live girl to a dead boy. I knew just such a thing as this would happen to me in my old age for a long life of cussedness. And what's more, I'll wager I'll never be able to give a great husky thing like you away. You cost as much to feed as a man. Who'd want you?"

But even as he stormed at me I felt his strong old arms cease from their tremblings and clasp me with a very rough tenderness.

"I do, General," said my Gouverneur Faulkner as he attempted to take me from that very rough embrace of my Uncle, the General Robert. "I'll take her off your hands."

"No, sir, I never ask personal favors of my friends,"

answered my Uncle, the General Robert, as he held me away from the arms of the Gouverneur Faulkner with a very great determination.

"General Carruthers," then said my beloved Gouverneur Faulkner as he drew his beautiful body to all the height that was possible to him, and looked into the eyes of my beloved Uncle Robert with his own, which are stars of the dawn, so that all of his heart and soul and honor shone therefrom in a radiance, "the Marquise of Grez and Bye went a three days' journey into the wilds of the Harpeth mountains with me to rescue my honor and for the welfare of this great State and of France. And because we thought not of ourselves but of the welfare of Harpeth and of France, and did but what was necessary as two comrades, God has revealed to us his gift of gifts - love. As you see, she is returned to you radiant and unharmed. Have I your consent to try to win her hand in marriage?"

For no more than a long minute my Uncle, the General Robert, gazed straight into the eyes of my beloved Gouverneur Faulkner, and then a very beautiful smile did break from under those white swords crossed above his lips, as he spoke with a great urgency:

"Would you like to take the baggage along with you to-night, Governor? Don't leave her here. I don't want a woman about my house. I can wake up the county court clerk for a license," he said with a fine twinkling of the eye.

"Oh, but all friends must forgive me my deception; and then must not a courtship of great decorum be made from my Gouverneur Faulkner for the hand of the lady whom he would make his wife?" I asked with an uncertainty as I looked from my Uncle, the General Robert, to my Gouverneur Faulkner.

"I'm sorry, sir, but I think the Marquise is right and under the circumstances I'll have to make a very public courtship, which out of consideration for you I'll make as ardent and rapid as possible. Only we three know the wonderful truth and we'll keep it to ourselves." And as he spoke that great Gouverneur Faulkner bent and laid a kiss of great ceremony upon the hand of Roberta, Marquise of Grez and Bye.

"Very well, sir, I'll keep her for a few days and have her fitted out in a lot of folderols for you, but only for a short period, mind you. A very short period!" answered my Uncle, the General Robert, with a smile that showed much delight in me. I flew to him and gave to him an embrace with my arms and also laid my cheek against his.

"I am for always your most humble and obedient girl, my Uncle Robert," I whispered to him.

"Humble and obedient - no woman would know those words if she met them in her own drawing-room," he answered to me with a great scorn but he also gave to me a shake that was of a seeming great fierceness, but that I knew to be a caress.

And into that caress came also another interruption of great hurry. My Buzz entered the door with a rapidity and this exclamation:

" What's the trouble, General? I just got your phone and -" Then he too stood in a great and sudden stillness, regarding me as I stood from the shelter of the arms of my Uncle, the General Robert, and looked into his eyes of great fright.

"My Buzz," I said to him softly.

"Great heavens!" he exclaimed, with terror in his eyes as he backed away from me. "I haven't had but one glass of draft beer, General."

"It's all right, Buzz," answered my very wise Gouverneur Faulkner, in a voice of great soothing. "This is just - just Robert in a - a -"

"Not much Bobby, that," answered my Buzz as he backed farther towards the door. "I think I'll step outside in the cool air. I haven't felt well all day. I - " and with which remark my good Buzz turned himself into the arms of the lovely Mademoiselle Sue entering the door.

"I'm tired of waiting out there in that car, Buzz, and -" And again came an awful pause of terror. But is it not that women have a wit that is very much more rapid than is that of men? I think it is so.

"You know, I thought Bobby was a queer kind of man and he is a perfectly lovely girl," she said as she came towards me with a laugh and her lovely arms outstretched. "I read about two French girls who got into Germany in German uniforms, just last night in a magazine. You are some kind of a French spy about those dreadful mules, aren't you, Bobby dear?" And as she asked that question of me, my lovely Sue gave to me a kiss upon my lips that I valued with a great gratitude.

"Please make it that my Buzz also understands," I pleaded to her within her arms.

"Brace up, Buzz, and be nice to Bobby, even if he is a girl. Just when did you begin not to like girls, I'd like to know?" questioned my Sue of him with a great emphasis.

"You see why it is that I cannot go into that business of timber with you and be married to -" I made a commencement to say to him.

"That will do, L'Aiglon," interrupted my Buzz with a great haste and a glance in the direction of lovely Sue. "Forget it! It is an awful shame, for you were one nice youngster and -"

"Be a sport, Buzz, and forgive her and - love her again," said my Gouverneur Faulkner with a laugh. "That is, as much as Miss Susan will -" But at this point my Uncle, the General Robert, caused an interruption in the conversation.

"What are you doing here, sir, when I left you to watch the side-steps of that French popinjay and the Whitworth woman? Did you hear what all that powwow was about at her tea fight this afternoon?" he demanded of fine Buzz, with a great anxiety. "There's been hell to pay, since you left, Governor, and I think this French scoundrel and Jeff's gang are preparing to put through some sort of a private steal if you jump the track on them."

"Madam Pat has got 'em all up at the Club, plotting in a corner at the little dinner dance we got up when his High-and-Mightiness refused the rural expedition, as soon as they heard you were not to go, Governor," said my Buzz with a great anxiety in his face. "I'd like to see anybody put out Mrs. Pat's light when she is once lit."

"It's all right, Buzz, and don't worry. Something has arrived to stop it all. It's up at the Mansion now and is man-sized," answered my beloved Gouverneur Faulkner with a great soothing.

And after that remark there were many very long explanations that made a beginning about the crooked back of the wee Pierre, which, in a letter come to my Uncle, the General Robert, that day, was declared by that great Doctor Burns to be of a certainty straight within the year, and that ended in the library where my Uncle, the General Robert, and my Gouverneur Faulkner, with good Buzz, read and read yet again the papers that my great Capitaine, the Count de Lasselles, had signed for an honest delivery of the many mules to France. I do not know all that my beloved Gouverneur Faulkner said to my Uncle, the General Robert, for I remained in the hall with my Sue in a discussion about the telling without offense of the departure of Robert Carruthers to my Belle and other loved ones. And to us soon returned my Buzz of great curiosity.

"There is no humbleness that I will not perform for their forgiveness, my Buzz and my Sue," I said to them. "Seek that they grant it to me."

"Oh, it will be so exciting and up-to-date with its spy and war flavor that everybody will forgive you. You are a lovely darling and they'll all be glad you are a girl - all the boys especially," said to me my Sue, with a defiance at my Buzz.

"Sure, Bobbyette, I'll see that you're no wall-flower," he made answer to her in the person of me, with a return of that defiance. "Come on, Susan, let me take you home. Good night, old top - no, I mean *belle Marquise*" and it was a very funny thing to see that Buzz with a great awkwardness, bend and kiss my hand at a laugh from my Sue as they left me.

It was not for many moments that I stood alone in the hall after the departure of my Sue and my Buzz, before there entered my beloved Uncle, the General Robert, and also my beloved Gouverneur Faulkner, who came to stand, one upon the one side of me and one upon the other.

"Sure you wouldn't like to take her along with you to-night, Governor?" again asked my Uncle, the General Robert, with a great fierceness but also a twinkling of the eye.

"Only as far as your garden for a few minutes, General," answered my Gouverneur Faulkner with that laugh of a boy I had remarked once before up in those mountains of Old Harpeth, and he took my hand in his as if to lead me through one of the tall windows out into the fragrant night.

"All right, take her and don't return her until you have to," remarked my Uncle, the General Robert, as he handed me in the direction of my Gouverneur Faulkner and immediately took his departure up the stairs.

And it was under the light of the old moon, in the garden of those *grande dames* Carruthers, that Roberta, Marquise of Grez and Bye, who is the last of their line, walked with the great gentleman who was and is her lover. Is it that those beautiful dead Grandmammas each planted her flowers in her own great happiness so that they would give forth a very tender perfume in which to enfold the wooings of their daughters then not come into the world? I think it is so, and I was thus enwrapped in their fragrance as I was in the arms of that great Gouverneur Faulkner.

"Now I am a truth that I do love you," I made answer to a question that was pressed upon my lips.

"His woman is God's gift of truth to a man," were the words that were heard by those listening flowers and Roberta, Marquise of Grez and Bye, who from a world at war had come home.

Choose from Thousands of 1stWorldLibrary Classics By

Adolphus WilliamWard
Aesop
Agatha Christie
Alexander Aaronsohn
Alexander Kielland
Alexandre Dumas
Alfred Gatty
Alfred Ollivant
Alice Duer Miller
Alice Turner Curtis
Alice Dunbar
Ambrose Bierce
Amelia E. Barr
Andrew Lang
Andrew McFarland Davis
Anna Sewell
Annie Besant
Annie Hamilton Donnell
Annie Payson Call
Anton Chekhov
Arnold Bennett
Arthur Conan Doyle
Arthur Ransome
Atticus
B. M. Bower
Basil King
Bayard Taylor
Ben Macomber
Booth Tarkington
Bram Stoker
C. Collodi
C. E. Orr
C. M. Ingleby
Carolyn Wells
Catherine Parr Traill
Charles A. Eastman
Charles Dickens
Charles Dudley Warner
Charles Farrar Browne
Charles Ives
Charles Kingsley
Charles Lathrop Pack
Charles Whibley
Charles Willing Beale
Charlotte M. Braeme
Charlotte M.Yonge
Clair W. Hayes
Clarence Day Jr.
Clarence E. Mulford

Clemence Housman
Confucius
Cornelis DeWitt Wilcox
Cyril Burleigh
D. H. Lawrence
Daniel Defoe
David Garnett
Don Carlos Janes
Donald Keyhole
Dorothy Kilner
Dougan Clark
E. Nesbit
E.P.Roe
E. Phillips Oppenheim
Edgar Allan Poe
Edgar Rice Burroughs
Edith Wharton
Edward J. O'Biren
John Cournos
Edwin L. Arnold
Eleanor Atkins
Elizabeth Cleghorn
Gaskell
Elizabeth Von Arnim
Ellem Key
Emily Dickinson
Erasmus W. Jones
Ernie Howard Pie
Ethel Turner
Ethel Watts Mumford
Eugenie Foa
Eugene Wood
Evelyn Everett-Green
Everard Cotes
F. J. Cross
Federick Austin Ogg
Ferdinand Ossendowski
Francis Bacon
Francis Darwin
Frances Hodgson Burnett
Frank Gee Patchin
Frank Harris
Frank Jewett Mather
Frank L. Packard
Frederick Trevor Hill
Frederick Winslow Taylor
Friedrich Kerst
Friedrich Nietzsche
Fyodor Dostoyevsky

Gabrielle E. Jackson
Garrett P. Serviss
Gaston Leroux
George Ade
Geroge Bernard Shaw
George Ebers
George Eliot
George MacDonald
George Orwell
George Tucker
George W. Cable
George Wharton James
Gertrude Atherton
Grace E. King
Grant Allen
Guillermo A. Sherwell
Gulielma Zollinger
Gustav Flaubert
H. A. Cody
H. B. Irving
H. G. Wells
H. H. Munro
H. Irving Hancock
H. Rider Haggard
H. W. C. Davis
Hamilton Wright Mabie
Hans Christian Andersen
Harold Avery
Harold McGrath
Harriet Beecher Stowe
Harry Houidini
Helent Hunt Jackson
Helen Nicolay
Hendy David Thoreau
Henrik Ibsen
Henry Adams
Henry Ford
Henry Frost
Henry James
Henry Jones Ford
Henry Seton Merriman
Henry Wadsworth
Longfellow
Henry W Longfellow
Herbert A. Giles
Herbert N. Casson
Herman Hesse
Homer
Honore De Balzac

Horace Walpole
Horatio Alger, Jr.
Howard Pyle
Howard R. Garis
Hugh Lofting
Hugh Walpole
Humphry Ward
Ian Maclaren
Israel Abrahams
J.G.Austin
J. Henri Fabre
J. M. Barrie
J. Macdonald Oxley
J. S. Knowles
J. Storer Clouston
Jack London
Jacob Abbott
James Allen
James Lane Allen
James Andrews
James Baldwin
James DeMille
James Joyce
James Oliver Curwood
James Oppenheim
James Otis
Jane Austen
Jens Peter Jacobsen
Jerome K. Jerome
John Burroughs
John F. Kennedy
John Gay
John Glasworthy
John Habberton
John Joy Bell
John Milton
John Philip Sousa
Jonathan Swift
Joseph Carey
Joseph Conrad
Joseph Jacobs
Julian Hawthrone
Julies Vernes
Justin Huntly McCarthy
Kakuzo Okakura
Kenneth Grahame
Kate Langley Bosher
L. A. Abbot
L. T. Meade
L. Frank Baum
Laura Lee Hope

Laurence Housman
Leo Tolstoy
Leonid Andreyev
Lewis Carroll
Lilian Bell
Lloyd Osbourne
Louis Tracy
Louisa May Alcott
Lucy Fitch Perkins
Lucy Maud Montgomery
Lydia Miller Middleton
Lyndon Orr
M. H. Adams
Margaret E. Sangster
Margaret Vandercook
Maria Edgeworth
Maria Thompson Daviess
Mariano Azuela
Marion Polk Angellotti
Mark Overton
Mark Twain
Mary Austin
Mary Cole
Mary Rowlandson
Mary Wollstonecraft
Shelley
Max Beerbohm
Myra Kelly
Nathaniel Hawthrone
O. F. Walton
Oscar Wilde
Owen Johnson
P.G.Wodehouse
Paul and Mable Thorn
Paul G. Tomlinson
Paul Severing
Peter B. Kyne
Plato
R. Derby Holmes
R. L. Stevenson
Rabindranath Tagore
Rahul Alvares
Ralph Waldo Emmerson
Rene Descartes
Rex E. Beach
Richard Harding Davis
Richard Jefferies
Robert Barr
Robert Frost
Robert Gordon Anderson
Robert L. Drake

Robert Lansing
Robert Michael Ballantyne
Robert W. Chambers
Rosa Nouchette Carey
Ross Kay
Rudyard Kipling
Samuel B. Allison
Samuel Hopkins Adams
Sarah Bernhardt
Selma Lagerlof
Sherwood Anderson
Sigmund Freud
Standish O'Grady
Stanley Weyman
Stella Benson
Stephen Crane
Stewart Edward White
Stijn Streuvels
Swami Abhedananda
Swami Parmananda
T. S. Ackland
The Princess Der Ling
Thomas A. Janvier
Thomas A Kempis
Thomas Anderton
Thomas Bailey Aldrich
Thomas Bulfinch
Thomas De Quincey
Thomas H. Huxley
Thomas Hardy
Thomas More
Thornton W. Burgess
U. S. Grant
Valentine Williams
Victor Appleton
Virginia Woolf
Walter Scott
Washington Irving
Wilbur Lawton
Wilkie Collins
Willa Cather
Willard F. Baker
William Makepeace
Thackeray
William W. Walter
Winston Churchill
Yei Theodora Ozaki
Young E. Allison
Zane Grey